A FUTURE FOR DISBELIEF

Philosophy in a Dehellenized Age with Implications for Theology

Allan M. Savage

D.Th., S.T.D., Litt. D.

I am disinclined to believe in the hidden power of the immanent divinities which, as Thales thought, all things are full of. Belief in the Christian God implies, so far as I am concerned, a positive disbelief in Fate: necessity be damned, for all I care. I refuse — let me make the religious nature of this act of un-faith clear, I refuse — until, if ever, I should be shown otherwise, to believe the primitive superstitions that there are implicit necessities within being, that being has, as its very reality, an inner warrant to command assent, and that invisible predeterminations constitute it and make it definable as that which has an antecedent call on the intellect.

(Leslie Dewart, *Religion, Language and Truth*, 1970:162)

DEWART'S BOOKS

CHRISTIANITY AND REVOLUTION: LESSON OF CUBA (1963)
This book is actually an essay in political philosophy addressing the relationship between Church and State. The lesson to be learned, from a theological perspective of pre-revolutionary Cuba, is that the Church may not remain spiritually relevant to the faithful as the traditional relationship between Church and State begins to end.

FUTURE OF BELIEF: Theism in a World Come of Age (1966)
This book concerns the daily experience of Roman Catholics at the time of the Second Vatican Council. The context reveals the issues and passions of the day. He shows a way out of the Hellenist cultural setting, while remaining faithful to the truth it has expressed.

THE FOUNDATIONS OF BELIEF (1969)
Will Christianity undertake to direct its own evolution or continue to evolve at an obsolete rate and in a pre-conscious mode? Dewart argues that the reshaping of the future is but the other side of the past. The dehellenization of Christian belief does not mean the rejection of the Hellenist past, it is not un-hellenization. The task to which philosophy is called today is to set dehellenized foundations that transcend metaphysical philosophy, varieties of which can still be recognized in our contemporary belief systems.

RELIGION, LANGUAGE AND TRUTH (1970)
The religious crisis of the Catholic Church has to do with philosophical questions that underlie theological and religious disputes. What are merely philosophical views have often been vested with the certitude of faith and the authority of revelation. We may take advantage of critical insights from human experience in order to improve upon our concept of God, religion, language and truth.

EVOLUTION AND CONSCIOUSNESS: The Role of Speech in the Origin and Development of Human Nature (1989)
Given Dewart's notion of dehellenization this book is a clear and useful presentation of his philosophical thought for contemporary philosophy. The deconstruction of one's inherited way of thinking is a threatening activity. As an invitation to philosophical growth, dehellenization is the conscious creation of the future of belief within an evolutionary context.

HUME'S CHALLENGE AND THE RENEWAL OF MODERN PHILOSOPHY (2016)
According to Dewart, modern philosophy stagnated because of the failures, which he tries to correct, of an earlier philosophical age. His attempts at correction are concerned with human sense perception and its truth content as understood within Western philosophy since its origin in ancient Greece. In order to clarify common sense through philosophy he focused on experience and understanding and the consciousness of the human mind which in turn led him to the cultural question of the contribution of Christianity to philosophy. This question ultimately became the foundation for his "dehellenization" of Western thought, the fruit of which is this book. Dewart has proffered a challenge for modern philosophy to further demystification of the "laws of nature." Modern philosophy needs to focus consciously on cognition, reality and causality to reconstruct the discipline and align it with what one's experience reveals.

Table of Contents

Foreword

An Introductory Note on Theology 1

Ab Initio 5

My Philosophical Life–World 9

    Holism: A New Approach 10

    Understanding God 11

    The Past or the Future 12

The Catholicity of Vatican II and the Church

of the Future 13

    Private Judgment: Catholic and Protestant 15

    Doctrine and Dogma 16

    The Spirit of the Christ 17

    Human Evolution and Salvation History 19

Further Thoughts on My Life–World 21

    Theological Understanding within the Church 23

    Meaning 25

    Thinking Theologically 26

    Dehellenization 33

    Future Considerations 36

The Dehellenization of the Future of My Belief

and Other Topics 39

       Culture 40

       Responsible Freedom 42

       Self–knowledge 43

       My Awareness of God 46

       Theological Dehellenization 48

       Self–differentiation 52

       Christian Status 53

Theology Outside the Theological Guild 56

Closing Reflections 61

Reference List

About the Author

Endnotes

Foreword

While Allan Savage is the author of thirteen previous books and numerous articles, I submit that this one is the most personal that he has written.

In this work, he allows us into his scholarly and inquisitive mind as he retraces his philosophical and theological background, sharing with us, essentially, his conclusions with respect to his personal, spiritual journey. Having found himself in a world being propelled forward by social, cultural and religious change and being unsatisfied with the answers provided by his classical formation, he came to find a home in existential, phenomenological philosophy. Within the Western school of scholastic philosophical thought, he viewed the answers to his questions regarding his personal, contemporary experience as rooted in a static past, one with authoritarian answers assumed to be relevant for all time.

Influenced by the *ressourcement* partisans of Vatican II as well as by the 'dehellenization' of Western philosophy advocated by his teacher and mentor, Leslie Dewart, Savage came to the conclusion that existential phenomenological philosophy provided a method by which his spiritual life was both revitalized and evolutionary. Here he is able to continuously construct his present and future lifeworld in which are incorporated his relationship with God and with his faith community.

I first met Father Allan when he was appointed pastor of St. Patrick's Parish in Québec City in 2000. Shortly after his arrival, we began a discussion group that met weekly. It soon became apparent that our discussions were not to be 'business as usual.' We were not simply to be re-schooled in the past or re-catechized. Through his persistent questioning, he enabled us to recognize where we were situated along our own spiritual timeline and how we got there. As a scholar in both theology and philosophy, he rooted our present in our past, returning us always to the revelation of the scriptural roots of our faith. It is fair to say that in this process I was sometimes escorted and sometimes launched, with the inevitable turbulence, into the future of my belief. While I was fully aware that the ground was shifting beneath my feet, it was not until much later that I realized that the axis of my spiritual world had tilted and that I was, indeed, in a different spiritual place. In some sense, the path through which Savage takes the reader in this book mirrors the one he led us through in those discussions.

I must state, for the benefit of the reader, that I am one of the 'untutored' in matters philosophical. For those who are similarly situated, there is much knowledge and insight to be gained from this book. I cite, as one example, the discussion of words ending in '-ism' versus those which end in '-ity.' If one examines this in specific reference to 'Catholicism' versus 'Catholicity' one understands how this provides the basis for a more expansive and inclusive spiritual vision. It reflects and explains his personal convictions with respect to ecumenism. In particular, it has influenced how I see myself in relation to the broader faith community of the People of God. I am very grateful for this new perspective. For the intellectually curious, *A Future for Disbelief*, has much to offer for reflection, opening up for the reader the possibility of new perspectives and spiritual growth.

Patricia Shallow
Québec City, 2017

An Introductory Note on Theology

Throughout this book, I cite theological examples of the changes in my philosophical thinking. For the reader's benefit, I present this introductory note on theology. The note is part of Chapter 5 (pp. 95-103) of Edward Schillebeeckx's, *Revelation and Theology*, which I have edited, in précis form, presenting it in his own words.

The term theology has, in the course of time, been applied with various meanings to different realities. Initially, the word was used with reference to the mythical stories of the gods. Theologians in this sense were the ancient poets such as Homer (12th to 8th century B.C.?) and Hesiod (circa 700 B.C.), who wrote theogonies, [i.e., genealogies of a group of gods], and told the myths of the Olympian gods. Theology, in this sense, was contrasted with meteorology which dealt in a more scientific manner with the divine heavenly bodies. Aristotle (circa 384 B.C.) spoke of theology as poetic myths about the gods. The view that these myths about the gods were simply a mythological form concealing true reference to God gradually became accepted. Plato (circa 428–348 B.C.) consciously dissociated the essential content of these myths from their mythological content. Aristotle also used the word *theology* with a new meaning or, at least changed its field of application. Making a three–fold division of science (*epistēmē*) into the physical, mathematical, and theological, he raised theology to the level of a philosophical science and made it the "first" form of philosophical thought. This "first philosophy" was concerned with the highest causes of the visible, divine, astral world.

The first sense [of the term *theology*] lay behind Aristotle's use of the word which meant 'to speculate about the gods.' Later, in the Hellenistic period (323 B.C.–31 B.C.) the word meant, in the context of emperor–worship, 'to venerate as a god.'

The word *theologia* acquired a new application in view of the swing towards cosmic religion. The deities were no longer the gods of Olympus, but [of] the cosmos itself – the *meteora*, or astral bodies. Meteorology had now become the sphere of theology.

1

These ideas persisted up to the patristic period. Augustine (+430) adopted the classic definition: "There are three kinds of theology, that is, of the discipline which is concerned with the gods: one of these is the mythic, the second is the physical, and the third is the civil." In this definition, the 'civil' kind of theology means the theology of public worship, the worship of the emperor as god. The term *theology* was Christianized very late [in history] because of the reluctance on the part of Christians to use pagan terminology. It was from the fourth century onwards that the Greek Fathers used the word *theology*.

The word *theology* was not adopted as readily by the Western church. Abelard (1079–1142) was the first in the West to consistently use the word *theology* in the Christian theological sense. In the tradition of Abelard, as in the Byzantine theology, the word *theology* tended to mean a treatise about God himself, rather than the theology of the mystery of Christ.

Aquinas (1225–1274) seldom used the term *theology*, and whenever he did so he used it in a very different sense from the sense in which we should use it now. The study of the human soul, because of its direct relationship with God, was called by Aquinas a theological study, whereas the study of the human body was not [called a theological study]. It is clear that the term *theology* did not have the full meaning in the scholastic period that it has today. It was in the period between Aquinas and Duns Scotus (1266–1308) that the word *theology* came to be used as the technical term for what had previously been known as *Sacra Doctrina*. It was especially speculative theology that was influential in bringing about this change from *Sacra Doctrina* to *theology*. The wide meaning which theology previously had was thrust into the background by a discursive procedure which had been adopted by theology and which had become a "science of conclusions." Thus, the classic term *theology* was placed in the category of speculative theology from the very moment of its birth.

Later, this had unfortunate effects. The *Sacra Doctrina* was divided in the modern period into all kinds of independent disciplines. Moral theology, towards the end of the sixteenth century, apologetic theology in the seventeenth century, and later dogmatic theology, that aimed to define the limits of revealed religion as distinct from all the questions discussed by the scholastics.

In order to establish the concrete structure of theology and its distinctive methodological procedures, it is not possible to proceed from the natural data of what scientific work is, whether these are the data of the Aristotelian scientific concept or those of the modern, positive, phenomenological, and "humane" sciences. The structure of revelation itself and the act of faith associated with it must suggest the type of reflection to which faith in Christ can lead. Only then shall we be able to throw light on the scientific structure of theology in all its many activities.

An Afterthought

Schillebeeckx's comments were published in 1967, at the time of writing when, it seems to me, that theology as ministry had not yet been recognized by professional theologians. However, a generation later, the seeds for such recognition were being sown by certain contemporary theologians and independent, educated minds. Among them I include Paul Trudinger. He says in a lecture in 1986:

> I have suggested that one of the most important tasks to which we are called as pastoral workers, as healers, is to foster amongst persons we relate to, *the practice of the presence of God* [my italics]. We should enable people to experience being enfolded in God's love. I believe we should give much more time and attention than often seems to be given in our ministerial and clinical training programs to help each other to learn to "to pray without ceasing." This is not to minimize the importance of other aspects of disciplined study and practice – in the case of seminary education, for example, of Biblical interpretation, of systematic and historical theology, of liturgics

3

and counselling.... We obviously cannot "say prayers" without ceasing. When *we* say prayers, *we* do the talking, as it were. ... No, we are little skilled in *realizing* God's presence [Trudinger's italics]

Thus, we can now include ministry and pastoral care to Schillebeecks's summation of "theology in all its many activities" expanding the understanding of theology in the experience of the contemporary faithful.

Ab Initio

I had wondered at times, beginning in my early adult years, and I continue to wonder today if there ever would be some kind of universal philosophical agreement, some kind of unity of philosophical understanding in the world. This book is my attempt to think through this many–sided topic and arrive at conclusions that satisfy me, at least up to this point in my thinking. Others, without a doubt, will need to arrive at their own conclusions. I think that for such a unity of philosophical agreement to be achieved, humans would need to surrender their unique powers of self–reflection and self–identity to some sort of universal uniformity constituting their nature, if such a thing were possible.

When, in my early adult years, I encountered individuals from various cultures who often held beliefs different from mine, as well as, differing beliefs among themselves, I was frequently frustrated by their differing opinions. However, by delving deeper into these differing beliefs, while in university, it eventually became apparent to me that Western philosophers favoured a particular interpretive perspective based on classical Greek philosophical understanding. In hindsight, I recall that this classical Greek philosophical understanding often left my questions needing further answers.

I am aware as well, that in those years there had been what amounts to progress in the sciences, but that nothing similar had occurred in philosophy. I wondered why science had advanced and philosophy had not appeared to advance. The answer to that question, I came to believe, was to be found within the respective methodologies and objectives of the disciplines of science and philosophy. Looking into the historical development of science and philosophy, I discovered that originally there was no distinct separation between the two. Initially, each discipline accepted the other as searching for the same thing, that is, the truth, although each was searching from differing points of view. In time, however, as history records, science did branch off from philosophy, and their respective methodologies did take on different founding principles and their terms of reference became mutually less understandable and acceptable. This resulted in Western philosophers deciding that philosophy, not being a system of proof–providing propositions, was not a science, but an art.

I recall that I was disposed to view the relationship between the two, not as antagonistic as some academics might, but as complimentary. I recognized that science and philosophy both provided answers to the deeper questions I had about life, but from different points of view. From my perspective, the data presented by the scientist provided the subject matter for the philosopher to contemplate, whether classically or phenomenologically. In other words, the goal of the philosopher is to seek the meaning of, and an insight into the facts that the scientist provides.

Unlike classical philosophy, however, phenomenological philosophy takes a different approach to meaning and cannot be taught as a system of thought, as has been done in the West with classical Greek philosophy. Rather, phenomenological philosophy must be personally experienced without the classical intent of searching to disclose an objective sought–after truth somehow contained within the facts. That is, phenomenological philosophy amounts to an interpretive stance that the philosopher adopts towards life, rather than a system of living to be embraced. As a phenomenological philosopher, then, I determine the meaning and significance of my experience from a subjective point of view, but not in isolation from the community in which I live. The meaning and significance of my experience and that of my community will be mutually understood through an inter–subjective awareness.

Scientific techniques are difficult to apply to the study of personal meaning and to the significance of one's life with any sense of authority or accuracy of interpretation. Nor can scientific technologies provide any theory to account for the meaning and significance of the life of a community. But since this is not the purpose of scientific technique, another discipline is needed to explain the meaning and significance of life. That discipline, I discovered, is phenomenological philosophy.

During my studies for the Bachelor of Arts degree, I soon realized that the classical philosophy of Western Europe could not answer the existential philosophical questions that arose in my experience. In short, classical philosophy presented a system of understanding that was inadequate for my contemporary experience.

As I see it today, instead of the classical method of philosophy, the phenomenological method of philosophy is increasingly being used to contemplate the meaning of one's personal existence in the world, even in an unconscious way in the day to day experience of individuals. But there is also conscious resistance in the Anglo–American academic culture to phenomenological philosophy. Also known as Continental Philosophy, and is somewhat rarely favoured professionally in the universities. I suspect that the dynamic of phenomenological interpretation is not often recognized as philosophy consciously undertaken by an individual. Rather, the dynamic appears as common sense until further reflected upon.

Scientific interpretation, as we know, requires narrow parameters restricted solely to demonstrable facts, which change in light of new discoveries. I see no such parameters or progress in philosophical thought as I see in scientific interpretation. In lieu of progress, I see in phenomenological thought a deepening appreciation of my personal life from an existential, as well as an evolutionary perspective. As I matured, rather than frustrate me, the varieties of philosophical perspectives that were open to me inspired me to undertake my own critique of philosophy. How I began this critique and arrived at my decision is the modest intent of this book. [1]

---

[1] I am thankful to Elizabeth Dewart, Leslie Dewart's daughter, for supplying me with a copy of her father's posthumously published book, *Hume's Challenge and the Renewal of Modern Philosophy*. Any reader familiar with the works of Dewart (1922–2009) will no doubt recognize his influence upon my thinking. I was taught by Dewart at the University of Toronto, in the early 1970's and since then I have written about the significance of his work

Checking the references listed at the back of this short volume, the reader will notice that the latest reference is dated 2008. This is deliberate. I have listed works that were introduced to me, for the most part, during my university years. Some I discovered later. Since then, I have continuously built upon these authors' philosophical insights and continue to do so right up to the present day. These texts have assisted me in developing a critical way of thinking as I sifted through and re–organized my thoughts.

As a rule, I have not cited exact references from any book. But, I have often paraphrased the thoughts of the authors whose works I have consulted. It is through the bibliography at the end of the book that they receive due credit for influencing the changes in my philosophical thinking.

Finally, as any reader will soon discover, I am presenting my thoughts neither in a conventional, nor a systematic manner. This symbol § and the corresponding heading in the text indicates a shift in the direction of my thought. This indicator should help the reader to make the transition from one notion to another more easily and make my ideas appear less disconnected, although they do remain partial in exploration and development.

elsewhere. (*Dehellenization and Dr. Dewart Revisited: A First Person Philosophical Reflection*, 2009, [2016])

My Philosophical Life–World

The question I ask myself in this book is: Am I experiencing a problem with the philosophical foundations of my knowledge? My experience of a world of scientific facts, as well as logical, rational relationships no longer satisfies my philosophical curiosity for knowledge about my life–world. There are various systems of knowledge available to me to explore my intellectual curiosity: philosophical, psychological, scientific, etc., but none of these systems has been able to adequately express the totality or complexity of the experience of my life–world. As I eventually discovered, however, I was able to express my understanding of my life–world more adequately through a phenomenological philosophy.

In my life–world, the sciences are required for a dialogue with philosophy, although it does not have to be a dialogue of equal partners. I have contrasted their respective methods of interpretation many times and I have found them both wanting with respect to the philosophical and scientific foundations for my knowledge, especially my religious knowledge. Although I found that my scientific knowledge fared much better, I am limiting my comments to a philosophical understanding as it pertains to my religious convictions.

Upon finding the traditional approach to my philosophical knowledge wanting, I converted to a phenomenological philosophical method of interpreting my experience. Given my religious convictions as a phenomenological philosopher, God is not the direct focus of my philosophy. Rather, the case is that I contemplate other phenomena than God in order to reach God, without God, as it were. According to Laycock (1986), this notion of reaching God without God was introduced by Edmund Husserl, (1859–1938), the principal founder of phenomenology. As I explain in this book, I use phenomenological philosophy to interpret my religious experience so that I can give meaning and significance to my life as the ancient Greek philosophers gave meaning to their lives in bygone ages. [1]

I recall that I experienced early on in my philosophical contemplation two significant phenomena. Firstly, that I had inherited my religious world–view which I did not make or design. Secondly, I also knew that I could not stop the philosophical evolution of my inherited religious world–view. As time went on, I came to understand that I was personally involved in the direction of its evolution to some degree. However, my world remained principally determined by the dominant notions of ancient Greek philosophy, notwithstanding any changes I was able to effect to any significant degree,

§

Holism: A New Approach

As a Western Christian I live, as many of the faithful do, with the anxiety and tensions felt in the religious and spiritual life that come with the end of conventional Christianity. Yet, within these anxieties and tensions I see indications of alternative approaches within philosophy that could lead to a different future. One is to abandon critical philosophy altogether and live a "wysiwyg" life–style; what you see is what you get. This would be a sort of fatalist approach to life which would be a return to the philosophical past. Another is to radically re-define or up-date classical terminology, a sort of philosophical *aggiornamento* which assumes that no real evolutionary change has occurred in philosophical concepts. To my mind, these alternative approaches arise, in fact, from the failure of classical philosophy at trying to discover the meaning of contemporary life. Among these approaches that could lead to a different future I have discovered the process of philosophical dehellenization which has enabled me, in fact, to consciously create the future of my belief. The shift in my understanding to a process of dehellenization ultimately led me to the theological realization that the Church of Christ, understood as subsisting in various denominations, does not exclude those who have been excommunicated from a visible Christian denomination. I

10

discuss more below about who is "in" and who is "out" of the church.

Presently, as I write this book, I contemplate my religious experience existentially, not speculatively, as I once did. That is to say that the world into which I was born has become my life–world. That is to say, my world of common sense understanding has become my life–world of existential understanding. By life–world I mean my conscious everyday world of immediate experience. I mean, in fact, Husserl's notion of *Lebenswelt*.

Through my existential contemplation of God, through my phenomenological philosophy, I consciously transcend the boundaries of my creaturely existence in such a way that I become more God–like, as it were. In becoming more God–like, then, I now understand myself through a holistic perspective, that is, through a transcendental perspective, wherein I am greater than the totality of all my individual parts. And, I do mean a *holistic*, not a *wholistic*, perspective. These words which are often understood as similar, or just a variant in the spelling of the same word are, in fact, not identical in meaning. More will be said about these terms below, but for the moment it is sufficient to understand holistic as denoting a phenomenological notion of the totality of an organism, and wholistic as denoting a classical notion of a total organism. The holistic understanding of totality reflects a core element within my life–world.

§

Understanding God

I come to understand God through the same process that I come to understand any other person, that is, through a mutual self–giving. This remains the case, even though phenomenologically understood, God is not one entity among others. Yet, God relates to me and I relate to God. As a believer, this relationship, for me, requires both a philosophical and theological understanding on my part given that God has been revealed within my life–world. However, as a philosopher and as a theologian, I recognize that philosophy and theology are different from revelation. In my experience, philosophy and theology originate with me and revelation originates with God.

As a phenomenological philosopher, I consider the possibilities, probabilities and actualities in my life–world. Thus, I come to understand about God indirectly through my philosophical attitude. As a phenomenological theologian, I contemplate the active presence of God revealed in the concrete phenomena of my life–world. Through a phenomenological attitude, I relate to God's active presence directly. In other words, through philosophy, I understand the gift; through theology, I encounter the giver, as it were.

§

The Past or The Future

As with any personal relationship understood phenomenologically, my relationship with God defies objectivism but not objectivity. Objectivism is a notion that belongs to Hellenized philosophy and which prefers to preserve the past. Objectivity, on the other hand, is a notion that belongs to a phenomenological philosophy that prefers to create the future. Thus, the challenge presented to me was either to be a custodian of the past, by remaining within a Hellenized philosophy, or become an architect of the future by consciously initiating a phenomenological encounter with God in my life–world. I discuss below more about a preserved past and a consciously created future. However, for the moment, it is sufficient to note that should I ever factor out my consciousness in the creation of the future of my belief, I will have removed that which differentiates me as a human being within the world. In choosing to create the future of my belief, as a human being within this world, I have come to realize that I am truly other and greater than the sum of my individual parts. The future of my belief involves the Catholicity of the church, not the Catholicism of the church of the future, which I discuss next.

The Catholicity of Vatican II and the Church of the Future

In addition to those academics who have a professional interest in phenomenological philosophy, I intend this book as a possible point of philosophical departure for any impulsive and untutored reader of philosophy who decides to undertake something different, thus challenging his or her mind with an unfamiliar topic. [2] With such individuals in mind, then, and without formal introduction to a theological perspective, I cut directly to the chase and present a particular issue for phenomenological consideration. I begin this chapter by contemplating the church as a mystery within the phenomenological Catholicity of Vatican II.

By introducing the notion of Catholicity, I distinguish speculative language from qualitative language. Speculative language belongs to classical philosophy, whereas qualitative language belongs to phenomenological philosophy. In the English language nouns with the suffixes "–ism" and "–ity," characterize classical and phenomenological language respectively. Funk and Wagnall's *Canadian College Dictionary* defines "–ism" as a suffix attached to nouns to mean "a distinctive theory, doctrine, or system: usually used disparagingly," and "–ity" as a suffix attached to nouns to mean a "state, condition, or quality."

The following terms, often used in discussions in philosophy and theology, illustrate this distinction; spiritualism vs. spirituality; materialism vs. materiality; personalism vs. personality; humanism vs. humanity; nationalism vs. nationality; historicism vs. historicity; Catholicism vs. Catholicity; individualism vs. individuality; modernism vs. modernity;

---

[2] I use the words *intend* and *intention*, or a variation of them, in the particular philosophical sense introduced by Edmund Husserl (1859–1938). That is to say that when I intend something, I am not merely planning or proposing something. I am also reaching out to something beyond the present moment of consciousness. I am pointing to a future, not yet realized, but with its roots in one's present consciousness. Thus, providing this book as a possible point of departure for the reader may achieve far more than I am aware.

dualism vs. duality; rationalism vs. rationality; moralism vs. morality; Deism vs. Deity, etc. But, it should be remembered that there are exceptions to this pattern. *Holism* is a phenomenological notion with no linguistic classical counterpart.

This short book, as a product of my philosophical contemplation, is not a chronological history of my religious thought. Nor is this book intended as a catechism as conceived in the schools of scholastic theology. Rather, it is a philosophical reflection intended to clarify for the reader, as well as myself, my phenomenological understanding and insight into pre–Vatican II and Vatican II philosophical concepts in light of the notion of Catholicity, not of Catholicism. Any philosophical clarification may then be applied to theological concepts.

As I choose to undertake my particular philosophical contemplation from within the church, I require membership in a community which is the *locus* of my contemplation since there is no philosophical insight possible in an isolated individual inquiry. My particular community is the Roman Catholic Church whose theology is currently supported by classical philosophy. An inquiry into the existence of the church, through the discipline of sociology, may provide religious knowledge of the culture, but I doubt that it can reveal theological meaning within the church. In other words, sociologists are not theologians and cannot access "the mind of God." (Truthfully, I have never met a sociologist who has made that claim.)

As a theologian, I have experienced the philosophical limitations of Catholicism as the classical understanding of the faith. But, I have also experienced the philosophical openness of Catholicity, which is the qualitative or phenomenological understanding of the faith. However, even though Catholicity is free from the objective limitations of Catholicism, it does disclose the contingent and subjective limitations of the person.

§

Private Judgment: Catholic and Protestant

Private judgment, as a philosophical stance within Christianity, had distinguished Protestant from Catholic theologians in pre–Vatican II times. To my mind, private judgment as a philosophical stance is no longer serviceable in distinguishing the Protestant from the Catholic theologian. Within an understanding of Catholicity, both Protestants and Catholics exercise private judgment in their theological interpretation. In the Victorian era, a convert to Roman Catholicism, George Tyrrell, (1861–1909), noted that the Protestant believer accepted scripture, given by God, as the supreme rule for belief. The Catholic believer, on the other hand, accepted the church as the supreme rule, given by God, for belief. Today, however, both Protestant and Catholic believers interpret the norms of their supreme authority, the scriptures or the church, through private judgment within their communities. That is to say that neither accepts their authorities without question. They both exercise their critical judgment. And in exercising critical judgment one has an opportunity for conversion from classical philosophy to phenomenological philosophy.

It still is the case today that it is to charismatic Christianity, as revealed in the New Testament, and not to the church as an institution that the Protestant believer looks for enlightenment by Christ. The Catholic believer, on the other hand, continues to look to the institution as a charismatically gifted community for guidance and enlightenment by Christ. The charismatic Christianity evident in the New Testament era reflected the initial period of inspiration and enchantment in the life of the church. As long as the conditions of individual inspiration and community enchantment were effective and in force, there was no need to form a particular organization or government for the believing community to enable enlightenment by Christ. That particular organization of government would appear later, as

15

inspiration and enchantment waned and the advancement of formal learning increased.

The scriptures, in which the Protestant faithful find their institutional roots, may be studied as any historical documents in light of the norms of textual criticism. Textual criticism discloses the literary conventions of the era in which the texts were written. In contemplating the history of literary conventions, George Tyrrell noted that we do not ask if Socrates really said what Plato puts into his mouth. Rather, we ask: Is Plato's Socrates the true Socrates? Did Christ do or say all that the Fourth Gospel ascribes to him? Is the Christ of the gospels the true Christ? I asked myself this same type of question in the early years of my philosophical career. I eventually concluded that the scriptures were not written as a chronological history and cannot be used as any sort of proof–text to establish Jesus' divinity.

Generally, it can be argued from the perspective of textual criticism that the New Testament has been consciously written to agree with the various Old Testament prophecies so as to present an *ad hominem* argument against the Jews for Christ's Messiahship. Furthermore, science acting as an independent, disinterested and private judge, cannot establish the truth of the scriptures. Thus, it is safe to conclude that private judgment is exercised in the experience of both the Protestant and Catholic believer.

§

Doctrine and Dogma

I no longer hold that all that the church taught about the theology of dogmas, sacraments and church government was accepted as fully known to Peter and the apostles, who in turn passed that knowledge on to their successors. In light of the historical investigations of the theology of the church I have rejected this pre–Vatican II view of the church. In short, given my insights into Vatican II I moved towards Catholicity and away from Catholicism in my theological understanding of the church.

To my mind, it is evident from the historical investigations of the late 1800's that church government has developed from a loose federation of democratic communities into a highly centralized and hierarchical structure in which all the teaching authority of the church had become centralized in the pope. This historical transition intrigued me and further investigation into church history helped me clarify my theological thinking. Many of the Catholic theologians of the late 1800's believed that the teaching authority of the church would never return to the ecumenical councils in which it ought to reside. At that time, there was a serious movement towards theological centralization. The schoolmen of the day equated the faith with theological orthodoxy and they assumed that Christ's mission was primarily a theological one. They argued that the church must necessarily possess the same authority which Christ possessed and demonstrated in his teaching and miracles. I soon came to realize that this classical view of the church's authority can only be maintained through a philosophical perspective that remains dependent on Hellenism. I began to wonder what a phenomenological understanding might reveal about the doctrine and dogma of the church.

§

The Spirit of the Christ

In accepting that the Christian revelation ceased with the death of the last apostle, the difference between Catholicity and Catholicism became a significant issue for me. I eventually concluded that Catholicity is primarily a way, or manner of life based on the example of Jesus of Nazareth. Alternatively, Catholicism is institutional living based on culture, which is not the way I prefer to interpret my life–world. Initially, George Tyrrell, mentioned above, experienced Catholicism as a fulfilling way of life which accounted for his conversion from Protestantism. He wrote, "I cared for it more as a life, and less

17

merely as a truth." [2] Eventually, however, he would discover that "truth" was more important than "life" to the Church of Rome.

Catholicity does not identify a body of doctrine given to the church about Jesus of Nazareth. Catholicism does that. Rather, Catholicity enables one to engage the spirit of the Christ as revealed through the Church. The spirit of the Christ does not reveal a body of doctrine about Jesus of Nazareth. Rather, the spirit of the Christ reveals its own presence to one's life–world. This being the case, my experience of the spirit of the Christ is readily susceptible to phenomenological understanding. Being active, the spirit of the risen Christ appropriates to its purposes those cultural experiences of the individual and community that are most suitable to establish its presence to the believer. From my experience, the spirit of the risen Christ uses the knowledge of the believer at hand to develop doctrine within the church. But this doctrinal development is not through propositions or formula. It comes via a conscious encounter with the same spirit that animated Jesus of Nazareth. In short, it comes via the enlightenment of the believer. Thus, the true teacher in the church is the spirit of the Christ acting immediately in and through the whole body of the faithful.

Reading the works of Thomas Aquinas, (1226-1274), who had a charismatic gift for theology, it often seems to me that the benefits of his particular theological insights are lost to many theologians today. Unfortunately, the version of Thomistic understanding, which dominates the official church's teaching today, often impedes the charismatic spirit that should animate the church's theologians just as it did Jesus of Nazareth. History and experience indicate to me that the spirit of Christ can act outside the official Church. It is possible for me to experience the spirit of the Christ outside the visible church, yet not outside the Church of Christ itself. To my mind, a phenomenological philosophy can disclose the theological understanding of what Vatican II intended when it affirmed that the Church of Christ subsists in the Catholic Church (*Lumen Gentium*, para. 8).

In this book, I am contemplating the church's theology in light of my experience in which a Hellenized philosophy no longer satisfactorily meets my needs. I live in an age of societal and cultural changes which are occurring throughout the entire world. Such societal and cultural changes have philosophical and theological implications for me. As Western society searches for a better world, often without seeking, either deliberately or inadvertently, a better philosophical explanation of its experience than the one it has inherited, it needs to re–assess its philosophical inheritance.

Ironically, this search for a better world has led some theologians to abandon not just their inherited philosophy, but also their faith. They become atheists with the positive intent of improving their lives and the lives of those around them. (Interestingly, it was only later in my philosophical life that I became aware that Christianity is the only religion to generate the notion of atheism.) Sincere atheists and anti–theists both offer a true challenge to religious believers. Louise Antony (2007) has edited a volume of personal essays from atheists that describes not only a valid alternative to religion, but also a fulfilling way of life, without God and apparently without the spirit of the risen Christ.

§

Human Evolution and Salvation History

An evolutionary notion of conscious human behaviour is replacing the static notion of the human individual as being a thinking animal. Initially, this evolutionary notion of human behaviour presented problems within my understanding of philosophy and theology, since I was then of the classical mind–set. Eventually, however, I decided that static philosophical notions which failed to satisfy me must be replaced by dynamic philosophical notions. This decision ultimately prevented me from accepting an atheistic point of view no matter how legitimate that point of view may have seemed to be to a mind critical of classical philosophy.

Human society is composed of a variety of cultures that give evidence for believing that human beings are destined for a

19

higher purpose in life. From a phenomenological point of view this higher purpose in life originates within the material world of incardinated individuals and not in a transcendent and ideal world of disembodied spirits. From the Christian perspective, humanity is at the centre of earthly life, yet, humanity may consciously extend itself beyond its incarnated limitations and boundaries. Both phenomenological and classical philosophy demonstrate humanity's ultimate purpose as being beyond itself.

From within the history of the people of Israel, and I mean their salvation history, has evolved the theological realization of the church as a phenomenological mystery. In our incarnated life as the People of God, we have come of age philosophically and now inaugurate the kingdom of God through a phenomenological belief in the mystery of the incarnation of Jesus of Nazareth. The spirit of the risen Christ has called into being a phenomenological community on earth constituted in faith, hope and charity. (And He did so without intending any historical or political governing structure. The variety of political governing structures developed subsequently to His resurrection.) The mystery of the spirit of the risen Christ, phenomenologically understood, constitutes a new understanding of the church within salvation history.

Further Thoughts on My Life–World

After World War I, a new Western world was born, as it were. However, as J. Middleton Murry (1927) notes, it was really not a new world but the old one clearly seen for the first time. It was a new world for those for whom the lines of demarcation were understood entirely differently from what they had seemed to be. This new world, at first, seemed cold, alien and hostile. Yet soon afterwards it appeared to have fresh hope as new insights were revealed and new lessons learned from a past and broken world.

And this is where I am today. That is, I continue to learn new lessons and insights from my past and somewhat broken, philosophical world.

Through a phenomenological understanding, I continue to discover deeper insights into the presence of God in my life–world. I have come to realize that it is not how accurate I am in my understanding that is important, but rather, how authentically I interpret my experience. In other words, I am not seeking the objective truth about my experience, but rather, I am seeking an authentic insight into my experience in contrast to an illusion or fantasy. In other words, I seek what is really real. And, any practical interpretation I make must be made in light of the philosophical changes taking place in Western society. As I contemplate the changes in my life–world, I see that a phenomenological philosophy is not readily accepted by many individuals. Not everyone accepts that the phenomenological method is one that satisfies and clarifies. To some, in fact, the phenomenological method dissatisfies and obscures the understanding of their experience. Yet, in my case it was the opposite. Over time, I came to the conclusion that scholasticism had somewhat hindered my thinking through introducing a dichotomous structure into my philosophical understanding.

I do realize, of course, that the defects of scholasticism are the defects traceable to its particular time and culture. And they are the defects of a philosophical language and speech that have not kept pace with modern experience. From my perspective,

21

even a revised form of scholasticism could not overcome these defects. The revised form of scholasticism to which I refer is neo–Thomism. Through neo–Thomism I was not able to satisfactorily interpret my experience. However, within a phenomenological understanding of my experience as a non–dichotomous unity, I was able to satisfactorily interpret my experience and thereby overcome the defects of scholasticism.

In my current situation, I contrast my present experience to my past experience and thus act accordingly to create my future of belief. Although this means that I must live within my inherited limitations, I need not be constrained by them. The truth is that I experience these cultural limitations in my life–world whether I like it or not. I cannot avoid them. However, I can be engaged, even if only partially, in transcending them.

In my life–world the interpretive task is perpetual and contingent. As an existential thinker, I know that there is no such thing as a final philosophy or theology. I conceive my work as different from the work of a theologian in the days when the great systems of the West were being constructed. As I see it, the task of both the contemporary religious philosopher and theologian is as follows. It is to make known the authenticity of reasoned belief in and about God to a new generation through a new philosophy, that is, a dehellenized philosophy. I find that the principle merit and usefulness of a dehellenized philosophy such as a phenomenological philosophy is its ability to satisfy the experience of the contemporary believer.

All philosophy is culturally influenced. Unlike classical philosophy, phenomenological philosophy does not conform, of necessity, to a given system of knowledge, methodology or norms of interpretation. Phenomenological philosophy is a conscious human understanding and as a conscious human understanding it can utilize any methodology for the purpose of interpretation. Any philosophy, even of the untutored sort, can provide some degree of satisfaction in religious interpretation.

History shows that natural theology, viewed by some as a type of philosophy and as a discipline in its own right, originated outside the Western Catholic ecclesiastical tradition. Natural theology, as a philosophy, is a proper way of inquiring into the world created by God rather than interpreting the revelation of God. St Thomas held this view, according to Schillebeeckx (1967). [3] As a theologian, I am required to interpret revelation within the *sensus fidelium,* that is, within the understanding of the faithful who constitute the church. As a social institution in this world, however, I believe that while the Church of Christ could get along without formal theologians, it could not get along without the *sensus fidelium.*

§

Theological Understanding within the Church

As I see it, much theological understanding within the community of the church arises through the insight, not of ecclesiastical officials, but of faithful individuals (*simplies fideles*) interpreting their experiences. The understanding of the faithful has often resulted in opposition to ecclesiastical officials whose role is to correct and modify the formal teaching of the church. Arriving at theological insight is a responsibility for the faithful to undertake according to Auguste Sabatier (2003). In their task of theological interpretation, they are to seek a contemporary understanding with respect to God's activity in the world, even if that role takes away from traditional understanding. If he is correct, the task of the faithful is nothing less than to assist in establishing new forms of theological interpretation within the Christian religion. He reminds his readers of this in *Religions of Authority and the Religion of the Spirit.*

Theology and revelation interact with each other. As a result, it has been my experience that theological understanding develops, and continues to develop, both on an individual and collective basis. My personal theological meaning, as it develops, is meaning that is significant for everyone in the community of the faithful. Thus, the degree to which the community and I can share our respective meanings establishes our degree of unity.

Since I am a member of the *sensus fidelium*, something more than a mere intellectual change occurs when I interpret my experience. It is an existential change, a change in the perspective of my life–world that allows insight into the authentic relationship between God and me. In my phenomenological existential understanding, such insight is not achieved through a more accurate understanding of theoretical knowledge. Rather, achieving insight is an act of intentionality, that is, my reaching out to the phenomena of others in my life–world so as to create religious as well as secular meaning in the practical order of life. In that reaching out to others my relationships are expressed existentially, and through those existential relationships I meet someone similar to myself. This may be another human being or an encounter with the presence of God.

It is almost a truism that when inherited gods die, most people do not become atheists. Rather, they invent new gods or return to the pre–theoretical gods of folklore. However, these new gods, or the gods of folklore, do not always prove to be a satisfactory replacement. Similarly, when inherited philosophies and theologies die, most people do not stop thinking philosophically and theologically. They turn to new philosophies and theologies or re–cast pre–theoretical folk notions in contemporary terms. In my case, turning to the new phenomenological philosophy rather than the classical one led me to new creative insights and relationships within my life–world. The case has been the same for my theology.

The controversial issues in theology, those introduced by the new scientific knowledge of the late 19th and early 20th centuries, were discussed in North America as pastoral or practical issues rather than theoretical ones. The reverse was the case on the Continent of Europe. There was more interest in theory than in practice on the Continent. From my phenomenological perspective, I highly doubt that scholasticism can remain as a suitable philosophy for the majority of the faithful, either in North America or on the European Continent.

The mission of the church is primarily salvific, that is, concerned with the saving of souls. It is only secondarily a mission for justice in the political and social order. In its primary mission, the church is not of necessity connected to any particular culture or philosophical system. Phenomenologically understood, the church transcends the temporal history of the People of God yet paradoxically, the church is mysteriously incarnated in its salvation history.

In its nature and mission the church is philosophically and theologically universal. Hence, in its universality it can function as a bond among communities of peoples as well as nations, provided these peoples and nations recognize and trust the church. It follows that these peoples and nations must guarantee the freedom of the church, allowing it to carry out its mission, according to Flannery, (1996). In a phenomenological understanding of the church, the priesthood of the faithful and the hierarchical priesthood, while distinguishable, are functionally and organically integrated. However, in the Hellenistic perspective these priestly offices differ ontologically. That is, they differ in their essence and being, and each is a particular temporal office and not a function.

§

Meaning

In the contemporary theological climate, there is an interest in the individual as a person from a psychological point of view. Diramuid O'Murchu, (2000), a noted Catholic author in psychology, seems to have had an experience similar to that of George Tyrrell, whose psychological understanding reflects a model of the psychological development of the person. Tyrrell's model of the psychological development of the person is in contrast to the clinical model of psychological development which often addresses pathological issues of personality. O'Murchu has written from a non–pathological perspective that his personal faith journey included many conscious transitions in which new ways of understanding superseded those which he previously conceived as unalterable or, according to official teaching, could never change and therefore should never be abandoned. Similarly, when I give meaning to my experience, I am not doing so merely as a person living in God's creation as a product of creation but also as an active agent, a co–creator with God and living in God's (our) creation. Obviously, I do not mean physical creation only. In giving meaning to my experience, I create my life–world one which exists independently of physical creation and which has its own standards of moral existence.

My ability to revise the meaning of my life–world as new data becomes available is possible because I am open to that which is transcendent. Being open to that which is transcendent connects me to the Other beyond myself. And I recognize that this connection adds a spiritual dimension to my life which is not mere metaphysics, and that I cannot separate my spirituality from my theological understanding.

§

Thinking Theologically

For any serious dialogue to bear fruit today in the life of the faithful, it must engage their personal and existential creative experience as well as their quantitative and qualitative understanding. At one point in the process of evaluating my inherited understanding, I related the thought of George Tyrrell to that of Leslie Dewart. I then compared their thoughts with my own classical understanding of that time. I have continued the task of comparing the thought of Tyrrell and Dewart to my own which still discloses fresh insights within my philosophical and theological thought. Given my own experience, I find it is unfortunate that, at this time in the development of Western philosophy and theology, the place of philosophy in relation to theology seems to have been usurped to a great extent by sociology and psychology. It is my hope that those readers who may not be philosophically inclined, but who gravitate to sociology and psychology, will discover new insights should they persevere with this book.

In the public forum today, theological and spiritual ideas are often perceived as needless. While in the private forum these may be accepted as necessary, phenomenological thinking distinguishes itself by serving as a means to disclose the proper origin of theological and spiritual ideas, whether private or public.

I detect that a shift away from the old style of competitive theological polemics towards a new style of ecumenical cooperation is taking place among contemporary theologians. For these thinkers, Western theology, which traditionally has been supported by classical philosophy, has shifted to a discursive theology which is often interpreted through phenomenological philosophy. It was within this context of a discursive theology that I began to make sense of my personal, though not necessarily private, experience. And in making sense of my experience, I found that I had to undertake a phenomenological approach to tell my personal story. Many theologians have had their stories to tell, including that of the convert George Tyrrell. In his day, and within his particular intellectual climate, George Tyrrell attempted to understand his religious experience through his philosophical contemplation of God's revelation.

As a theologian, the revelation of God is a particular focus in my life. My theological preoccupation has its roots in the Roman Catholic theological views that were in vogue in the early 20th century, particularly that of the *Nouvelle Théologie*. Ahead of his time, George Tyrrell's way of thinking reflected an ecumenical model of theologizing rather than the conventional polemical model of theologizing that was dominant in his day. It was through his model of theologizing that I found the beginnings of fresh insights into my faith.

One intention in this book is to draw the reader's attention to the fact that many creative and insightful contributions from theologians are often quoted and discussed by academics and other professionals. These academic reviewers and professionals often truly believe they have understood, and correctly expounded the ideas of these insightful and innovative theological thinkers. And in most cases, they probably have done so, but not always. George Tyrrell's story of creative and innovative theologizing is a case in point. The appreciation of his style of creative and innovative thinking is not as well recognized as it could be among professional theologians. The majority of academics discuss Tyrrell from an historical perspective, often within the (so–called) Modernist Crisis in the Roman Catholic Church. The extensive bibliographies compiled by M. J. Weaver (1981) and D. Wells (1981) in their books support my claim. However, David Schultenover, (1981), a critic of Tyrrell, focused on a different understanding rather than the conventional historical one. Schultenover wrote of Tyrrell's way of thinking that it is an intellectual history which is to be distinguished from a social history. Schultenover aimed to describe, not the Modernist Movement, but the intellectual development of a major contributor to that movement by focusing on the man and his thought.

Two modern developments are crucial in giving some rationale for the creative tensions that exist within the Western philosophical and theological traditions. The first is that medieval Christendom has come to an end and secularism exists in its wake. The other development is that a psychological understanding of the person has taken the place of the scholastic understanding of the person. If speaking of God really means that I am at the same time saying something about myself, then talking about God in categories that belong to an earlier cultural age simply cannot satisfy me.

One of the criticisms of Modernity is that it sets up a false confidence in rationalism and science. Given their ability to categorize and explain human experience rationalism and science, are often portrayed as being able to convey the totality of one's experience. Once I realized that this could not be the case, that neither could convey the totality of my experience, I undertook a phenomenological approach which directed me away from the dichotomous understanding contained in rationalism and science. The phenomenological approach permitted me to undertake a non–dichotomous, active engagement with my life–world in determining the future of my belief. In light of that engagement, I am of the belief that science poses a problem primarily for my philosophical interpretation of my life–world and only secondarily a problem for the interpretation of my faith — if at all.

The sociological entity in which I experience my spirituality is the church. Exploring all the various understandings of the church is a specialized discipline within theology called ecclesiology. The differing interpretations of the scriptural texts by the various denominations, plus the political, philosophical, and historical reform movements among the faithful have all contributed to a diverse self–understanding of the church. From a phenomenological philosophical perspective, the church is not a social arrangement imposed on the faithful. Rather, the church is disclosed as a communion of communities constituted by the faithful, each with its own self–understanding, history, culture and tradition.

There is a variety of expression in the church reflecting a variety of local cultures. In this regard, my contention for many years has been that the theological problems of the churches, within their varying local cultures, are first philosophical problems and need to be addressed as such. Afterwards come the theological solutions to the problems of interpretation of God's presence in the world. As I indicated earlier, I began forming this view during my undergraduate years when I studied philosophy and was introduced to the theological perspective of George Tyrrell, (1861–1909). Further, the philosophical insights of one of my professors at St Michael's College, University of Toronto, (Leslie Dewart, 1922–2009), motivated me significantly in consciously forming my convictions. It was Leslie Dewart's understanding of "dehellenization," a philosophical concept which he did not present as a negative concept meaning "unhellenization," that provided an opportunity for me to begin to evaluate my inherited classical understanding.

Contemporary theologians, those who theologize formally on behalf of a believing community, are required to think as professionals, as it were. However, pre–modern society and culture was not oriented to professionalism but to authoritarianism. The hierarchical order is the required form of any authoritarian organization structured for absolute rule and governance. Contemporary society and modern religious organizations are oriented toward professionalism, democracy and the principle of personal creativity. Within the churches of the Reformation, democratic governance is clearly evident. For the hierarchical churches, both Catholic and Orthodox, the principle of subsidiarity fulfills the intent of democratic governance.

My philosophical contemplation suggests to me, at least, that a phenomenologically understood church reveals a new ecclesiology that is based upon relationships among the faithful, not on an order of political government. Based on relationships, government becomes governance. Present day churches, in the Catholic and Orthodox traditions, are based on the notion of territorial jurisdiction. However, there is an option for the future governance of the church through an organic ecclesiology, one not merely territorially re–ordered, but one that is reconstituted phenomenologically. To my mind, such an ecclesial reconstitution requires, on a continual basis, that I reappraise the development of my Christian theology. This is so because I am living in a culture that has not been envisioned or brought about only by one factor. My present culture is determined by many factors. Among them are physical, metaphysical, mental, human, and divine causes. Indeed, my present culture may even be over–determined by a combination of these and other factors. By "over–determined" I mean no one factor can be held responsible for the direction of the cultural development of the world in which I encounter the presence of God. I take this to mean that, in truth, God is not solely responsible for everything that happens to me, or happens in the cosmos for that matter.

That is to say that I have a responsible role in the interpretation of God's revelation. This responsibility allows me to conceive of myself as a responsible co–agent in, and as a responsible co–creator of my society and culture. With this status, I am able to work towards building the kingdom of God on earth in light of a faithful interpretation of the revealed presence of God. Thus, the Kingdom of God is not to be politically understood as in the classical sense. Rather, it is to be existentially understood from a phenomenological perspective. My co–participation in the divine creativity is the risk that God has taken with me. I am conscious that this risk anticipates possible failure. There is a prophetic remark, attributed to Alfred Loisy, (1857–1940), about such failure: "Jésus annonçait le Royaume et c'est l'Église qui est venue." (Jesus came proclaiming the Kingdom and what arrived was the Church.) [4]

The Catholic institutional understanding of the church is as old as the first epistle of St Clement, (circa 75–110), in which the church is conceived as a divine institution. According to St. Clement, the church is an institution with officers whose duty is determined by an official status within the institution. In this understanding, the officers of the church are analogous to officers of the state. To my mind, Jesus of Nazareth would never contemplate endorsing any form of church government patterned on a model whose leaders were analogous to the state. It is clear that the apostles believed that the end of the world would occur within their lifetime, yet they made no provision for an institutional church as we know it today. The spirit that animates the church today is the same spirit that animated Jesus of Nazareth. In my experience, this same spirit reveals an understanding of Catholicity, not Catholicism, in the church today.

As a person with an indeterminate future, I am also an individual being who desires to evolve beyond my present self. However, if I, as a Christian, look at the world and understand it through Hellenistic eyes, I will find it necessary to look to the past and not beyond myself to find the meaning of my experience. In looking to the past through Hellenistic eyes I am tempted to permit the power of God to govern me. If I do permit the power of God to govern me, I remain a creature with no opportunity to evolve to a co–creator status. However, if I see the world phenomenologically, I look to the present and future simultaneously and I am able to establish a new relationship wherein God and I cooperate in both my present and future life, given my status as a co–creator with personal self–governance.

Given my phenomenological understanding, the transcendent God beyond me does not have absolute power over me in the classical sense. Rather, God's power is shared with me in my status as a co–creator. The fundamental relationship between God and me does not consist of a hierarchical relationship of power. It consists, rather, in a relationship of mutual presence in a conscious unity within my life–world, wherein I have become a co–creator, sharing in the divine power in creating the future of my belief. Thus, as I dehellenize my belief, I recast the meaning of my faith in terms that do not imply God's absolute power over me.

Contemporary theologians, both Eastern and Western, are beginning to realize that the present structure of church government which reflects classical theism must change. The present governing structure of the church is based on a territorial notion and not on a gift of God's grace or on divine charism. A territorial notion is an obstacle to the ecclesial governance of the church today. Note that I say "ecclesial governance," not "ecclesiastical government." And, as such, it will continue to be an obstacle in the future. Such territorial notions often do not conform to one's lived, that is, one's existential social condition, or life–world. Mine included. Further, it would be a theological error to promote the idea of a universal territorial super–church composed of all the faithful based merely on the philosophical notion of human political expediency.

It must be remembered that while individual humans do exist, a universal humanity does not. Furthermore, humanity as an abstract notion, is expressed through a variety of philosophical, political and cultural patterns. God is conceived as immanently present or absent in these philosophical and cultural patterns. When I conceive God as immanently present, I relate to others within my life–world so as to disclose a new and meaningful philosophical understanding which replaces the old one. New wineskins for new wine, as it were.

Victor Segesvary, (2003) reminds us that humanity, understood as an existential community of individuals, is too large an entity to be the bearer of a single shared culture. In this respect, the contemporary world is not that different from the world of the ancient cultures. It is, however, urgent that I find creative ways to interpret what is unique in the experience of my present life–world.

In returning to the sources of my faith, it is more responsible for me to promote a reasoned phenomenological philosophy rather than retain a culture of folklore in which to interpret my experience.

Psychology, sociology, history, anthropology, etc., contribute to my interpretive task, to some degree, but it is only philosophy that is in a privileged position to support my theological reflection. As a contemporary theologian, my task is not to look for an opportunity to prove through polemics a doctrinal point of view. Rather, my task is to express, to clarify and deepen my existential understanding of the faith for myself and for the community.

§

Dehellenization

Having come to appreciate the influence of Leslie Dewart in my academic career, my intention as indicated earlier, is to provide for the reader a reflective account of the development of my own philosophical thinking from my undergraduate years to the writing of this book. I have deliberately and consciously undertaken this reflective account. My motivation is to offer this reflection in the public forum because there may be other theologians or philosophers contemplating doing the same and may be interested in knowing of my experience. I present this reflection not as a chronological or historical sequence of events detailing the stages of my philosophical development. Rather, I invite the reader to revisit and reconsider his or her own thinking in the context of philosophical development. Thus, identifying dates and occasions marking the various philosophical movements of conversion when I stopped believing "that" and

33

began believing "this," is not my intent here. Rather, I consider those occasions when a series of conscious realizations converged in my thinking which presented a phenomenological moment of insight that changed what I believed. My personal understanding of philosophy, which is sympathetic to that of Plato and Plotinus, is that philosophy is an intellectual and contemplative activity. Furthermore, this intellectual and contemplative activity relates me to my environment from which I differentiated myself. This intellectual and contemplative activity has provided insights that have allowed me to organize and re–organize my theological understanding on a continuing basis.

Like many other students of philosophy throughout history, I began my questioning during my undergraduate years while studying classical philosophy which I later came to reject. During these years, however, there was not an immediate and total rejection of classical philosophy. In practice, I took what "worked" from classical philosophy and rejected what was irrelevant to my experience at that time. Today, unlike my undergraduate years, any rejection of what is irrelevant in my philosophy is more thoroughly thought out. What is relevant is consciously maintained. Over time, I have come to agree with Christopher Macann (1997), from a philosophical perspective, it is not that phenomena reveal or disclose being or even what it means "to be." Rather, the opposite is the case. Being, or what it means "to be" discloses or reveals phenomena. I no longer consider the legacy of Hellenistic philosophy as the necessary philosophical substrate common to all human thinking and experience. I once thought that to be the case, however. Now, I recognize that classical Hellenistic philosophy is only one point of view within an evolutionary process of philosophical traditions that constitutes human thinking.

Like many philosophers in the Catholic tradition I sought contact with, or knowledge of a metaphysical reality, that is, God through transcendental philosophy. At one time, Neo–Thomism seemed to satisfy my quest. In the initial years of my philosophical thinking, I accepted uncritically that what was truly real was enclosed *a priori* in formal ideological structures, that is, my experience was best understood as interpreted through Platonic idealism. I later came to realize that my experience neither revealed nor confirmed that such structures even existed. I had presumed them to be there. Eventually, and largely due to Leslie Dewart's philosophical influence, I accepted that there are no *a priori* structures to reality. Thus, I abandoned classical understanding and undertook a critical self–reflection on my experience.

My critical self–reflection opened up a new perspective, enabling me to understand and make sense of my experience. It was my arrival at this stage of critical self–reflection, according to Stöckl (2007), that marks the moment I consciously entered modernity. The notion of modernity, as a philosophical concept, refers to the experience of modernization and to the critical reflection upon this experience. Modernity, then, was the context in which I found myself engaged in the task of having to make sense of my experience. Once I understood this, I came to question seriously whether or not the scholastic philosophical idealism that I inherited from my Western culture did exist independently of my consciousness. I concluded that it did not. Rather, it is more accurate to say that I intentionally construct my ideas, or notions, through a conscious awareness of relationships with the world around me.

In my reflections, I note that I am able to distinguish between my being and my becoming, yet I am not able to separate my being from my becoming. They are, in my experience, one and the same. As well, I am conscious that my being and my becoming constitute a unity which leads me to understand them as equi–primordial. That is to say, from a dehellenized point of view, my being was always present.

§

Further Considerations

Within philosophy there are two sets of terms not to be confused. The terms "subjectivity" and "objectivity," are not to be confused with the terms "subjectivism" and "objectivism." They are not interchangeable. The former are phenomenological, that is, qualitative terms. The latter are scholastic, that is, quantitative terms.

Platonic, and some neo–platonic philosophers continue to subscribe to ideal forms in interpreting sense experience. Yet, they do not admit of any reality to the relationships among these ideal forms. This understanding is not consistent with a phenomenological perspective. As a phenomenologist, I admit to an existential relationship among entities since I see no reason to continue to hold to the existence of platonic material forms. That is to say, reality is relational rather than ideal in the classical philosophical sense. I have adopted this position because my conscious awareness does not analyze being and consequently discover a framework of material forms. My conscious awareness recognizes that all entities, be they living or non–living, are related among themselves.

Being conscious, I differentiate in my relationships between that which is "me" and that which is "not me." I am aware of my conscious self, that is, "me," as manifested through my body yet differing from my body. I am also aware of "me" as differentiated from other physical and non–physical entities. In short, I am not my body. Neither am I a spirit or non–physical entity separate from my body. Rather, as a human being I experience myself to be an incarnated entity in relationship with other entities, be they incarnated or not. By incarnated, I mean that I am an "in-the-flesh" living entity possessing a soul. Whether this soul is immortal or not is another matter that does not concern me here. As a human incarnation, I exist in such a way that I can relate myself to myself as well as to others. As a human incarnation, I do not experience myself as a dichotomized being, united through a joining of a body and a soul originally separate, but rather, I experience myself as an individuated being, originally unified, or constituted as body and soul, capable of being present to others as "me."

In my dehellenized understanding, I have recognized three unique moments of insight, or moments of conscious realizations within myself. They are: 1) the realization of my capacity for reflexive thinking, 2) the realization of my individuality that I am "this" and not "that," and 3) the realization of my personal integration. And I continue to become more deeply aware of the legacy of these moments as my conscious understanding deepens.

My relationships are realized through a conscious differentiation in my experience in which I distinguish between "me" and "not me," and not through any *a priori* determination imported from outside of my experience, that is, from any pre–determined idealism. Through my relationships, I am conscious that I exist, not only for myself, but also for others. It is within my relationships with others that my self–disclosure occurs. In this self–disclosure, I become aware of myself as an individual. As an individual, I am able to place myself in an appropriate relationship with my environment, and other living beings, of whom I have become conscious and from whom I am differentiated.

I, as a person, do not have the structure of an object. Rather, I am a person constituted as being greater than the sum of my individual parts. That is, I am holistically constituted as an incarnated individual person. The fact is that I am devoid of any fixed or final human construction, but not devoid of being perpetually constituted as human as long as I am alive. Human construction is a metaphysical concept, whereas, being constituted as human is an organic concept. It is through my organic constitution that I am able to determine an appropriate relationship with my environment and the universe from which I have consciously differentiated myself.

Through this process of differentiation, I become conscious of the temporal and the transcendental aspects of my existence which are co–terminus with my individuated being. In short, as a person, I am constituted as a unity and not as a union, of immanence and transcendence which makes me who I am.

The Dehellenization of the Future of My Belief and Other Topics

I undertake the organization of the future of my belief from within a dehellenized understanding. A dehellenized understanding is not a fixed understanding It is a process of the deliberate re–evaluation of experience that is perpetually undergoing development and re–constitution. It is a dynamic process. The dehellenization process helped me to recognize that my Christian and secular experience had been, for a time, the same. I had no need to distinguish between them. It was easy, therefore, for me to think that to be a Christian meant accepting uncritically the Western social and cultural order that I inherited. It took some time for me to realize that my social and cultural order was, in fact, the legacy of a Hellenized philosophical tradition.

Reading the works of some contemporary Western philosophers, I realized that this Hellenized philosophical inheritance was a serious commitment on their part. When they realized that the Hellenized philosophical and cultural inheritance was undergoing critical assessment, they often wrote rebuttals in favour of the classical approach. Realizing their bias, I ceased to follow their lead and rejected their efforts at rebuttal and sought instead to review critically my experience and develop a dehellenized approach to my philosophical thinking.

Engaging the Catholic philosophical language at the time of Vatican II, I favored *ressourcement* over *aggiornamento*. I favoured a return to Western philosophical sources, the result of which was not merely the updating of philosophical language. It brought philosophical language into conformity with modern usage [5] In light of Vatican II, as a philosopher and theologian experiencing the end of a classical philosophical age, I pondered what was to be my philosophical role in any new understanding arising out of my Christian and secular experience. My conclusion was that only a return to, and critique of the sources of Western philosophical thinking could provide a satisfactory start for me to readjust my thinking.

The cultural and social contexts in which I live are organized on the basis of a collective interpretation of the experiences of my community and myself. In the contemporary Western context, such organization is occurring slowly and I have realized that I am among those Christians who call for a collective interpretation based on experience. However, I am not taken seriously by many of my contemporaries. If I am taken seriously by some, I am not heeded by others. Their lack of interest, I believe, is due to their philosophical bias which favours an *a priori* belief pattern which they have retained from a Hellenized philosophical perspective.

In my philosophical contemplation, I soon realized that if answers to my questions were given to me beforehand by well–meaning, authoritative predecessors, there was no need for me to undertake any personal critical investigation with respect either to my experience or the accuracy of their authoritative answers. I could have remained philosophically passive and accept uncritically their ideas. But, I soon realized, that rather than simply accept my intellectual inheritance without question, I needed to accept my own intellectual responsibility and become an agent for change within myself and then within my environment. Thus, my problem became not just how to update my past understanding but, more significantly, how to plan for the future of my belief free from a Hellenized philosophy. I concluded that I could only plan for a future that was not a repetition, or variation, of my past experience and way of thinking through a methodology, one not dependent on a classical inheritance, but constituted phenomenologically.

§

Culture

In reflecting phenomenologically upon my experience, I have come to understand that Christianity is not an abstraction. Nor is it an ideology. Upon abandoning these understandings, I began to express my Christian belief phenomenologically through relationships within the culture reflected in my community of faith.

The faith community in which I live is an historical reality, not only in the social, psychological and natural sense, but also in the transcendent, spiritual, and supernatural sense. I must explain this. To believe in the Judeo–Christian revelation is to believe that my existence is influenced by certain events involving God's activity in the world. Even though I am conscious of God's activity, immanently and transcendentally in my experience of being and becoming, what I have found to be very significant is the realization that all my experiences could have been other than what they were. I was not fully aware of the implications of this insight until I was exposed to Leslie Dewart's thinking on the same subject.

Prior to this stage of my philosophical development, I had not managed to formulate a satisfying approach to the integration of Hellenic philosophical concepts into my experience. I think that part of the reason for this failure was due to the fact that Hellenistic cultural concepts were not merely unsatisfactory in interpreting my experience, but they were also foreign to my experience. In other words, my experience was not culturally Hellenistic. The philosophical and theological questions raised within my ordinary experience had little in common with the Hellenistic cultural and philosophical understanding which was beginning to be characterized as an age that no longer existed. Eventually, as I recognized that an alternative approach was needed, the question became one of interpreting, through satisfactory and contemporary concepts, my daily experience of the presence of God in my life–world.

The question of a satisfactory and contemporary interpretation replacing these waning Hellenistic cultural concepts is an existential, not theoretical question. In fact, within my new insight of existential understanding, contemplation did yield satisfactory results. One result was that I was free from the burdensome and inordinate influence of Hellenistic philosophy which had once been dominant in my life. In my earlier years, I had assumed that culture, which included my philosophical understanding, was somehow determined by pre–existing ideals. Today, however, my philosophical contemplation reveals that culture is as indeterminate in its organization as are the individuals who create the culture. Culture is neither an abstraction, nor a fixed ideology. It is a dynamic human activity reflecting my existence. It was through a phenomenological understanding that I was able to understand my culture as evolutionary. That is, as being evolutionary in the way human beings are understood as evolving.

§

Responsible Freedom

There are certain cultural constraints that determine my choices. Necessity, however, is not one of them. Events can be other than they are. Yet, even within the limiting conditions of my life–world, I have the capacity to make it other than it is. If my theological construction has any meaning and Christian value for me and my community, it is because I am trying to work out a proper relationship in order to live in responsible freedom. Responsible freedom is not license to do or believe whatever I desire. Responsible freedom is the freedom through which I respond to others and all that is real, which, in fact, limits me. Further, living within responsible freedom, I believe that I am to live in a philosophically contemplative manner which includes responding critically to the supernatural vocation to which God calls me. I try to respond creatively and faithfully to this call albeit in a dehellenized manner.

I have noticed that when Hellenistic philosophers claim to live in responsible freedom they often presuppose the role of fate. On the contrary, I am a believer not in fate, but in creative freedom. When, in creative freedom, I contemplate what I should do in organizing my future, I intend to include an understanding of what does not yet exist or is not yet present in my understanding. That is, I allow for the possibility of future alternatives to which God may be calling me. I incorporate the vision or insight that God reveals to me within the phenomenological understanding of my life–world. In short, I allow for the notion of an "open" future as opposed to a "closed" future in my life–world.

As a free agent, I am able to contemplate philosophical issues before acting on them. Thus, I am truly responsible for my conduct. No one else is. There is no group or individual who can cancel out my freedom. I can, however, surrender my freedom. But in surrendering my freedom, I would become dehumanized, that is, I would act like a robot. My free choices arise out of a creative capacity which is uniquely a human power. I cannot, therefore, surrender governing myself reasonably and autonomously and still remain human. As human, I am a creatively constituted person in body and spirit. In my creative freedom, I do not undertake efforts, as did Plato and Aristotle, to conform to an ideal order of reality. In other words, through my philosophical contemplation, I have come to realize that I freely organize my future of belief as an incardinated, individuated and dehellenized human being.

§

Self–knowledge

From early Hellenic to modern times, various philosophical traditions have asserted that human beings are merely thinking animals. Yet, I find that in my philosophical contemplation, I exhibit a peculiar and unique ability that I do not share with non–human animals. I am constituted differently. I am a being who is capable of understanding myself to be uniquely present to myself. The real difference between non–human animals and me is not that I possess a higher degree of knowledge. The real difference between non–human animals and me is that I am able to reflect upon myself and know that I am reflecting upon myself. If I ask: does the fish know it is a fish and the cat know it is a cat, etc., the answer is that I have no reason to believe that they do.

As my consciousness develops I am aware of a deepening of the knowledge of myself as a reflecting agent. A deepening of the knowledge of myself as a reflecting agent ultimately reveals the presence of a transcendental reality, that is, the presence of God in whose image and likeness I am made. As well, a deepening of the knowledge of myself reveals a deepening of the knowledge of God. In short, the deeper my self–knowledge, the deeper my knowledge of God.

What is unique and distinctive about my transcendental knowledge, as compared to my temporal knowledge, is that my transcendental knowledge takes the form of a qualitative as opposed to a quantitative understanding. My temporal understanding occurs within a quantitative experience. That is to say, my experience is in time. As well, given that my transcendental knowledge of God develops qualitatively, I become more aware of that of which I am already conscious, even if in an underdeveloped or imperfect manner.

My transcendental knowledge is an awareness of that which is real, which is outside time and does exist, but not as any form of being which is within time. As my consciousness of transcendental knowledge increases I realize, that is, I make real that which had always been present to me and which I have come to understand in a new light. Thus, in my transcendental knowledge, I recognize a sharper, clearer, and nobler meaning to my life in the presence of God. This new meaning is not the once hidden, pre–existing meaning now revealed. Rather, this new meaning has evolved out of an earlier meaning that I had incorporated unsatisfactorily into my life from my Hellenic inheritance. As it happens, I experience my transcendental consciousness as part of the continuum of my temporal self–knowledge that perpetually evolves and discloses itself as the presence of God.

To know a thing better, in traditional Western philosophy, often means to know more about the same thing. That is, knowledge is conceived quantitatively, not qualitatively. Such understanding became problematic for me when I understood that at the closing of revelation, after the end of the New Testament era, it meant that the Christian religion could not reveal any new truths. It meant that revelation could only increase through the multiplication and variation of concepts about the faith that were somehow already known. However, this understanding was not in keeping with my experience. I did not experience God's self–revelation in Jesus of Nazareth as limited to the various conceptions about the faith in a closed system of revelation. I had no sense of being restricted to knowing only an historical record of past revelation that had occurred and been completed in the past. On the contrary, I have experienced and continue to experience the living, open–ended revealing presence of God in my daily life.

Naturally, my theological understanding occurs within the experience of my particular religion. Further, my Christian theological organization is reflective of my belief. I have a personal history which distinguishes me from both other Christians and non–Christians and their personal histories, even though we all are made in the image and likeness of God.

As I mentioned earlier, I was not satisfied within the Hellenic approach to understanding the transcendent reality within my life–world. I am satisfied, however, with my conscious and continuing attempts at self–differentiation within that reality in which I was originally constituted as a unity, but not as a union. My self–differentiation within that reality continues as an active process whereby my unique identity emerges and is present to others as well as myself. Thus, I continue to conceive of my identity through that ability for self–differentiation which distinguishes me from other sentient beings. For me, to be a person, is to know myself in God's presence and to know that I know my presence to God. My personality is a manifestation of my unique self at any given stage of my conscious growth in my life–world. Further, I experience myself as an entity who desires to go beyond myself in order to deepen my self–knowledge.

§

My Awareness of God

I accept as historically accurate that the Hellenization of Christianity was the outcome of a gradual transformation of earlier cultural forms into later ones. Thus, Hellenism is not the cultural form of the world today. It was, however, the cultural form of the ecumenical world of the apostolic and patristic ages. Throughout the apostolic and patristic ages, it was practically impossible to distinguish between the universalization of Christianity and its Hellenization of Christianity. Contrary to the Hebraic philosophical perspective in which God is a presence of one kind among other kinds, from the Hellenist philosophical perspective, God is a transcendent being. Within my phenomenological understanding, one which is conducive to the Hebraic approach, God is that reality in and from which my being comes "to be." In other words, my unique life is a differentiated, or more accurately, an individuated life, coming–into–being and manifested through a relationship to God who is present to me. In the early stages of my philosophical career, I had accepted that there was truly a separation or a dichotomy between the essence and the existence of an entity, including God. I now entertain another understanding based on my experience, one which is not in accord with my previous Hellenistic understanding. As an existential thinker, my belief is grounded directly upon the experience of the presence of God and not upon ideas or concepts about God. That is to say, ideas or concepts about God do not confirm my belief in the presence of God. Rather, my experience is that my consciousness directly confirms the reality of God who is not a being among other beings but yet is present to me.

This knowledge of God as being present to me, however, does not result in a union of me and God. Rather, my knowledge of the presence of God comes about through my differentiation from and individuation in that reality – God. Paradoxically, God is "not me," yet there is that of God in me. Differentiation is a process in which my existence within time means that I must consciously create myself, that is, differentiate myself within and from the reality – God. The reality – God, which is beyond the physical, is revealed to me as an intangible presence through the process of differentiation. The fact is that through the process of differentiation, I am conscious of being in the presence of reality such that when this reality is felt by me, I am more authentically fulfilled than I would be were I not conscious of it.

I experience my individuality through a holistic consciousness. That is, I am conscious that I am more than the sum of my individual parts. A holistic consciousness does not burden me with having to prove that there is actually a God. Rather, I am preoccupied with understanding how the reality, God, is authentically present within my consciousness and reciprocally how I, in my reality, am present to God. My preoccupation is with the presence of God, not with God's existence. Thus, through a holistic understanding, what I realize or make real in my life–world is God's presence to me rather than God's existence. It is truly the presence of God that makes me greater than the sum of my parts.

It is to be remembered that the phenomenological presence of God is not the ideal presence of God as understood in Hellenistic metaphysics. If I look at the world and understand it through Hellenic eyes, I will find it necessary to concede God's power over me and possibly against me. Through experience, however, I am conscious that God does not have power over me in any negative sense. I am conscious, as well, that the fundamental relationship that exists between me and God renders us present to each other. This, I believe, is a true conscious insight realizable to all human beings. In my daily life, as I dehellenize my Christian belief, I recast the meaning of my faith in terms that do not imply God's dominance over me.

In accepting Hellenistic philosophy, I had agreed to God's dominance over me through trying to do his will. In my dehellenized understanding, however, the perception of a supernatural, transcendental being dominant over me is not an intrinsic part of the Christian faith. What is now intrinsic to my

Christian faith is the conception of the presence of God to me as gift. In other words, the presence of the giver is the gift.

As Western philosophy departs more and more from its Hellenic roots, the concept of inherited supernaturalism loses its usefulness for contemporary philosophy. However, mainstream Catholic philosophy has remained supportive of its inherited supernaturalism and is rather unsympathetic to any immanent spirituality phenomenologically understood.

I have become aware of an alternative stance to the scholastic view that grace builds upon my human nature. The alternative stance is that my human nature develops in the presence of God because that is how I, as human, have been constituted — to grow in the grace of God.

§

Theological Dehellenization

Concerning dehellenization and belief, one question that I have asked myself is whether or not I consciously undertake to critically construct the future of my belief or, do I choose to remain satisfied with a pre–critical understanding? This is the question I now address. In my phenomenological philosophical contemplation, I consider issues from a meta–metaphysical perspective. That is, having rejected traditional Hellenistic understanding and having accepted a phenomenological philosophical perspective, I have transcended Hellenistic metaphysical understanding. That is to say that phenomenological understanding does not contain any variation of a classical metaphysical understanding. Rather, phenomenological understanding addresses the existential phenomena of one's life–world, not the idealism of a speculative philosophy. Thus, in phenomenological philosophical understanding, the real problem is not whether the world will change or whether it will remain the same. The real problem is whether the world will change of its own accord, without my participation, or whether it will be changed deliberately, consciously and with my participation.

I participate existentially in changing my world through relationships understood phenomenologically. These relationships define the limits of my life–world and my participation within reality. While there is no possibility of returning to the fixed nature of the past, the shaping of my future of belief does require an analysis of the circumstances of the past without a re–living of them. In analyzing my past, I am conscious of myself, not as a static being, but as an active free agent in the presence of other active free agents, including God. In organizing the future of my belief, I have chosen neither a traditional nor any updated philosophical perspective such as Neo–Thomism. It was through learning to define myself in terms of phenomenological philosophy that I came to appreciate the rationale of the process I was using to construct the future of my belief.

Any philosopher who assumes that every entity is necessarily constructed as a self–contained unit rejects the possibility of any dynamic activity of growth and remains within the static Hellenic mind–set and closed to an open future. In organizing the future of my belief, the opposite is the case. That is, I intend the dynamic actions of reflecting, engaging and growing while remaining open to the future.

The dehellenization of my belief does not mean the rejection of Hellenistic philosophy and the substitution of another more appropriate philosophy as if the two had not been related. The term dehellenization is not a negative term, that is, it is not un-hellenization. In positive terms, I experience dehellenization as the conscious creation of the future of my belief. Reviewing my intellectual history, I have come to understand that the task which awaits me is not the dismantling of one metaphysical system and reconstruction of another system, but rather the transcending of all metaphysical systems. In other words, my task is meta–metaphysical. My task is not only the transcending of Hellenic metaphysics which is but one understanding to be transcended. My task is, in fact, the transcending of all philosophical metaphysics thus reaching out to that which is real.

Given his context, it is understandable that St Thomas thought that the scholastic way of thinking was the only way to think. However, I am conscious of the fact that there is no necessary context or methodology that I must employ in philosophizing about that which is real. As well, there is no philosophical methodology that is natural or privileged in understanding that which is real. My life–world is one of increasing personal responsibility. My problems are those, characteristic of finding an appropriate intellectual and philosophical methodology for the interpretation of this responsibility.

A phenomenological methodology has the advantage of incorporating, not just my intellect or ability to reason, but my entire personal experience in the act of believing. As I reflect on my personal experience, I become conscious that my knowledge of my contingency is insufficient. I attempt to overcome this insufficiency, however, through a conscious holistic understanding. A conscious holistic understanding is rooted in my desire to find meaning within my life. Since I live in a community of faith, the problem for me becomes whether or not I must presume any reason for or concrete expression of my faith to be applicable to everyone. The answer is no. While I am conscious of my particular creative freedom, I must not presume that the degree of my creative freedom is required of all. There is a difference of degree in the creative freedom of human beings. Others will have the unique experiences and outcomes of their faith in seeking meaning. Through my phenomenological understanding, I realize that the outcome of my freedom is not predetermined, as I once thought. I am not a fatalist. That is why I consciously and freely attempt to create the future of my belief, understood holistically, through the theological virtues of faith, hope and love.

Because of the dissatisfaction with the philosophy I inherited, I now embrace a philosophy that is suitable to my increasingly mature theological thinking in order to give proper expression to my understanding of God's relationship with me. This is my theological crisis.

My theological crisis has to do with the epistemological and metaphysical questions which traditionally grounded Western theology and belief and which I inherited. In short, my theological crisis is philosophical. Therefore, my philosophical need is for a deepening of consciousness rather than for more information. A philosophical deepening of consciousness requires a re–conceptualized understanding of the relationship to my faith community and the world. In the process of a philosophical deepening of consciousness or re–conceptualization, what I am conscious of is not that phenomena manifest themselves as real but that reality manifests itself as phenomena.

I am conscious that in expressing my dehellenized theological understanding, I employ language personally but not privately. When I think, or talk about my life–world, I also create an essential relationship to the concrete world at large. In this relationship, I do not merely relate to my life–world and the concrete world at large, but I self–relate to my life–world and the concrete world at large. In my thinking, I become related to the concrete world at large as a self, that is, as a subject who knows of his relationship to his life–world and the concrete world at large. Thus, what I achieve in my language and thought is the creation of myself, of my identity through relating myself to both my life–world and the concrete world at large.

The creation of myself is not done, however, by extracting truth from the experience about myself and duplicating it through a process of representation. Even though an insight may be the same for every philosopher, the remembrance of it is not, of necessity, the same for every philosopher. Remembering is that characteristic of consciousness which accounts for the fact that the more I actually know, the more I potentially know. Thus, when I remember anything, I enlarge my conscious horizon or awareness. Consequently, if I were to accept uncritically any pre–given conceptual and cultural form of theological remembering I would be preventing any enlargement of my conscious theological horizon or awareness. Accepting the pre–given form of theological remembering characteristic of

Hellenism obscures any meaning which it once may have revealed and my theological crisis would not be resolved. Thus, I require my theology to be dehellenized.

§

Self–differentiation

A challenging philosophical concept within contemporary Catholic theology is that of conceiving humanity as *homo faber* vis à vis that of humanity as *homo creator.* That is, man the maker vs. man the creator. My response to this distinction is to understand myself as "man the creator" rather than "man the maker." (Although at times the latter does apply.) That is, rather than receive my "tools," I create them in order to intend my future. I have rejected what I experienced to be an inadequate scholastic philosophy and have accepted a new methodology for the creation of the future of my belief. In reflecting from a "that was then, this is now" perspective, I came to realize that an evolutionary understanding of the world was not available to the Hellenists. This evolutionary understanding remains a defining characteristic in my life–world.

In this evolutionary process, I re–create or differentiate myself by adjusting to my life–world and the given world at large through phenomenological philosophy. It is a characteristic of sentient life that adjustment to the given world is mediated through the senses. Further, in my life–world and in the concrete world at large I not only sense others, I also relate to others whom I recognize as being in the process of becoming or evolving, and who conceive of themselves as selves and me as a self.

As an individual human being I am not the centre of the universe. I do, however, experience myself as part of both an organic evolutionary universe and a techno–architectural universe. As did the Hellenist philosophers, I too participate in the cosmos. Their cosmos, however, excluded the modern technological and evolutionary aspect of modern culture. Hellenist philosophers lived in a different world, one which lacked the modern advantage of evolution and technology. They reflected on their particular cultural experience of the human condition. Unlike the ancient Greek philosophers, phenomenological philosophers, myself included, reflect on our own experience of a co–creative evolution of being and becoming in the universe.

To my mind, co–creative evolution manifests itself as a global phenomenon. As I arrive at each new level of consciousness within a co–creative evolution, I deepen my understanding. In this process, however, I experience nothing in the universe that tells me that the universe has been organized to satisfy or fulfill my needs or desires. Through my philosophical contemplation, I have no experience that any order or harmony of the universe is intended for my sake as a human being. Yet the revelation of God tells me the opposite. The universe is made for me. Revelation tells me that I am a steward of creation. Further, I conceive that I am more than a steward of creation. Having been made in the image and likeness of the creator of the universe, I share in the creative powers of the creator of the universe. Thus, as a co–creator in the universe, I ought to be faithful to myself and intend, in the presence of God, an order and harmony of the universe conducive to my own needs and preferences and that of my community. As a phenomenologist, I do not hold to the view that a parallel or alternative world independently exists. There is only one world. This world, the one in which I now live is constituted of my self–differentiated life–world and the concrete world at large. That is to say, the conception of any "other world" is really part of "this world."

§

Christian Status

Within the course of my reflections for this book, I came to realize that major cultural changes have caused me to accept that a new philosophical age has appeared in human history. This led me to recognize that I am an agent of some of these cultural changes, albeit of minimal influence. As I matured philosophically, my understanding of my inherited culture had become somewhat problematic for me. This was particularly due to the influence of Vatican Council II in which I began to discern the presence of God through the understanding of *ressourcement* and *aggiornamento*. [3]

One problem arising from the understanding of *ressourcement* and *aggiornamento* is how to identify, within phenomenologically philosophy, the Christian individual in the community as opposed to the Christian individual as traditionally identified in the church. Within the phenomenological understanding of the church of Vatican II, recognizing an individual as "in" or "out" of the church became a challenge for theologians after the Council. As I see it, they have managed to address this challenge to varying degrees of satisfaction.

Those theologians subscribing to the notion of Catholicism rather than Catholicity, for example, understand that bishops alone are the successors to the responsibilities given to the apostles. Traditional bishops delegate some of this responsibility to the priest and deacon in a hierarchical structure. Given our contemporary ecclesial experience, I suggest that this hierarchical structure, while true, is more authentically understood today phenomenologically rather than scholastically. The phenomenon of hierarchical authority, as understood in Catholicity, is not ecclesiastical and is to be preferred to the political structure of hierarchy as understood in Catholicism. Credit must be given to those bishops who have become motivated to present the church's teachings phenomenologically.

As one of the new People of God, I desire a philosophical and theological understanding appropriate to my experience. This includes a philosophical attitude which leads me to self–discovery and where I responsibly see for myself and responsibly do for myself in God's felt presence. In failing to see God's presence, I fail to "see" or "do" for myself. Since I undertake my

---

3. *Ressourcement*: a return to the sources, which implies less centralization by Rome; *aggiornamento*: the process of bringing an institution or organization up to date. Some Catholic theologians consider these as opposing terms.

self–discovery within a Christian community, I can clarify my particular insights in light of the community's insights.

Such inter–subjectivity reveals to me that God is ultimately differentiated from me, other individuals and the given world. God is wholly other, without contingency and not dependent upon me. I, however, am contingent and dependent upon God. Furthermore, through the inter–subjectivity of others in the Christian community, I participate in the mind of God. Better still, I participate in the presence of God, just as God partakes of my mind and presence. This is my Christian status.

As a theologian, I can never complete my philosophical and theological tasks. However, in these tasks I need to embrace a philosophy that will reveal the appropriate theological expression of the meaning of the revelation of God to me. In my experience, the most appropriate philosophy in revealing this theological expression for me is existential phenomenology. Existential phenomenology makes it possible for me to reflect upon myself and the revelation of God in a manner that was not possible within scholastic philosophy.

Theology Outside the Theological Guild

Formal scholastic theology began as a professional activity within the universities. Its purpose was to serve the church in clarifying and formalizing doctrine and dogma. On the contrary, I contemplate theology outside any formal ecclesiastical guild that is committed to an institutional, political or polemical agenda. I contemplate theology as an ecclesial enterprise in the context of a community of faith, not as an ecclesiastical enterprise. The term *ecclesial* refers to a concrete communal relationship among the faithful. The term *ecclesiastical* refers to the historical governing structure of a Christian community. [6] The doctrine and dogmatic formulations of the traditional Christian denominations are the result of reflections on the controversial theological interpretations of the church throughout its history. As a believing community, the early church needed to settle the controversies among the various theological opinions circulating in the local communities at the time. As a consequence, various doctrinal and dogmatic additions have accrued to theology over the centuries. In fact, these hindered theological reflection, and led to a religious understanding that did not always reflect or agree with the experience of the faithful.

My experience has been that my theological consciousness, which is my understanding of doctrine and dogma, underwent development in response to shifts in philosophical thinking. These shifts in philosophical thinking changed my theological understanding. Thus, the way I now conduct my theological thinking is through critical reflection and outside a theological guild. Critical reflection is an innate activity of the human mind that reaches into the depths of experience and consciousness. It seeks insight into existential questions arising within the shifts in philosophical thinking.

I think critically in order to create a future that will empower me to evolve authentically as human within my milieu and denotes a more biological being. Critical reflection allows me to transcend the social, political and religious experience and understanding that I embraced originally within a theological guild. As well, critical thinking discloses that philosophical and theological systems are not absolutes in themselves, but, according to Thomas, (1938) are contingent upon the culture in which they arise. Thus, critical reflection on my Western philosophical heritage reveals a movement away from supporting a publicly civil and ecclesiastical structure towards a personal and ecclesial community.

Friedrich Schleiermacher was among the first to recognize this phenomenon of a philosophical change from one system to another. He believed that, philosophically speaking, humanity is a self–organizing, pre–theoretical phenomenon whose laws are not simply the laws of social or scientific mechanics. According to Brandt (1941), pre–theoretical humanity acted according to its spirit which is manifested in religious and ethical movements such as holism and emergent evolution.

By reflecting on holism and emergent evolution outside the theological guild, I avoid the baggage of the political and power–related controversies of the church that emerged in the Reformation/Counter–Reformation period and which are no longer relevant. By reflecting outside the theological guild, a new *locus* for fresh investigations into my religious experience is opened up to me.

Thus, throughout this book the phenomenological understanding of my life–world has served to interpret that new *locus*. As a result, I continue to search for new and meaningful ways to reflect upon my religious experience outside the traditional theological guild. In my thinking, however, I cannot ignore the contributions of those other critical thinkers who have helped in shaping my past understanding. For me, their legacy exists, not by virtue of its own independent right, but because of its significance to my thought as a contemporary philosopher and theologian. Thus, my critical phenomenological reflection must take into account the legacy of artists, musicians, novelists, poets and psychologists. Of course, I must engage the legacy of the theologians whose critical phenomenological reflection has included the scriptures and personal accounts of their religious experience, particularly within the holistic perspective.

The holistic perspective discloses that an entity is other than and greater than the sum of its individual parts. That is to say, in holistic thinking, an entity discloses meaning beyond its concrete or phenomenal limitations. Within a holistic understanding, there are no limitations to the understanding of one's life–world. Within a holistic understanding, the horizon of my consciousness is unlimited. Within a holistic understanding, I seek to discover the wisdom inherent in the relationships among entities that constitute the human and divine milieu.

The purpose of my book is to introduce the inquirer to the evolution of my theological thinking. I do not intend to produce a theology that will be applicable to all people in all situations and cultures. My intention is to offer a model for critical thinkers wanting to act as their own interpreters, as Schillebeeckx (1984) has suggested. Of course, this model is offered within a community of believers and not meant to be followed in isolation.

My point of departure for writing this book is, in fact, rooted in the first part of the conclusion at which Charles Davis arrived after writing his book, *A Question of Conscience,* in 1967. "I can see well enough that the fundamental intellectual problems for Christians today are the problems of our knowledge of God in relation to modern philosophy and the question of the uniqueness of Christ in the confrontation with the other world religions." [7]

The process of phenomenological reflection is a descriptive rather than deductive process. The starting point for phenomenological reflection is the concrete human condition. Phenomenological reflection interprets experience in relational terms that undergo change and not through pre–determined norms that are not subject to change. Thus, the purpose of a critical phenomenological reflection is to criticize constructively the ideological, sociological and psychological attitudes found in one's life.

In spite of the emphasis given to the ecumenical dialogue that began in the modern world, Reformation and Counter–Reformation polemics continue to exist. Because of these polemics, many Christians who participate in the life of their respective denominations often feel that they are alienated from the Church of Christ. Remember that from a dehellenized point of view, the Church of Christ subsists, not only in the Catholic Church, but in the various denominations as well.

Scholastic philosophical thinking must present God as transcendent and outside of creation. Phenomenological thinking, however, discloses the presence of God, as immanent in, yet transcendent to creation. That is to say, when I think creatively, I feel the presence of God as immanent in, and yet transcendent to my life. In thinking creatively, I discover that I think and, consequently, act in co–operation with that which is "other and greater" than me yet is present to me.

As Fabel, (1983), concluded from his scientific synthesis of Teilhard de Chardin, the destiny of the universe, including its human component, may well be controlled by the life that arose within it. As an individual human being, I am aware of a greater purpose than to be confined to my biological life within the universe. That greater purpose is to think and love within the hopes, aspirations and anguishes of my age — all outside the theological guild.

For the purpose of thinking outside the theological guild, I propose that readers consider two distinct *loci* in their phenomenological reflection; the one concerning themselves and the other concerning their community. When conceived phenomenologically, the individual and the community are in a reciprocal relationship. Individual thinkers will present individual theologies and these theologies, in turn, will influence the experience of others. Such diversely presented theologies often develop negatively into a collective understanding or dogma. These arise from like–minded individuals and appear to be universal. As history has shown, such dogmatic confessions, appearing to be universal, have often later become merely normative for both the individual and for the particular Christian community.

Narrowly focused, particular Christian communities do not present a universal system of philosophical thought of the type that was attempted in the scholastic tradition characterized by

Thomas Aquinas. These particular Christian communities often embrace a biblical method of interpretation which appears to be universal. It is, in fact, narrow and particular.

The scholastic method is one of integration. This held together up to the middle of the 20th Century, when the culture–shattering events of the two world wars, the technological revolution, rapid developments in philosophy, psychology and the advancements of the social sciences and the humanities brought an end to medieval Christendom. Out of the end of medieval Christendom emerged a new philosophical way of thinking which now shapes the interpretive hermeneutic, that is, phenomenological philosophy.

For Catholics in particular and Christians in general, Vatican II symbolized the end of a conventional understanding of the faith and introduced a new approach to the hermeneutics of the faith through a phenomenological and critical understanding. Vatican II was not merely an up–dating of doctrine and dogma, an *aggiornamento*, but rather a phenomenological interpretation of a *ressourcement*, that is, a return to understanding the sources that ground Christian belief.

In general, two movements or identifiable trends characterize a phenomenological understanding of *ressourcement*. One is a return to and a reflection upon the patristic and medieval sources of theology. Another is a return to and a reflection upon the theological writings of St Thomas Aquinas. A third may be added; to return to and reflect upon the new philosophical movements of the late 19th and early 20th Centuries. Such reflection will need to consider Modernity and liberalism as understood within the holistic philosophical perspective. And it is this dialogue that has dominated my concern in this book.

Closing Reflections

Obviously, no philosopher is ever completely original. (However, according to Patricia Shallow, poets are.) Since philosophy has a history which reflects the perspectives of various thinkers, the idea of philosophical originality is practically a contradiction in terms. As a philosopher, I live within an historical current of Western thought and thus incorporate something of the history of my predecessors into my own thinking. In reviewing an earlier age in theological thinking, I recognized that many present–day problems of current Western philosophy are simply the logical outcome of the so–called Modernist Crisis of not–so–long–ago. As I mentioned previously, I contemplate the process of re–constructing a Christian theology from a phenomenological point of view. Therefore, in fashioning my life–world, I enter both the philosophical and theological intellectual world which I have inherited, as well as the concrete world from which I have differentiated myself. This means, however, that I am in dialogue with but one world understood from two points of view rather than two different worlds.

I have contrasted phenomenological theological understanding with classical or traditional theological understanding which is inordinately influenced by Hellenistic philosophical concepts. Therefore, I follow the insights of a dehellenized philosophy as suggested by Leslie Dewart, which presents a new philosophical perspective through which I interpret my theological experience. Drawing on his insights, I have focused in this brief book on the way my belief has been and continues to be shaped by relational understanding. Hence, "roles in relation to," instead of "goals as an end," are the subject of my attention. This means in the process of my theological contemplation, I need to pay special attention to the verb "to be."

For, linguistically and philosophically, "to be" means to be "some thing," that is, an entity joined to or connected with an underlying ideal form. In Western thinking, a philosophy of "to be" is a dichotomous philosophy which has become intrinsic to

Western theology. This dichotomous philosophical presumption is rendered unnecessary in a phenomenological understanding. Converting to a phenomenological understanding is a difficult task for many Western philosophers and requires a significant effort at sustaining one's conversion. Intuitive understanding suggests that the way things usually present themselves is independent of one's intention, and things are seen to be there whether we want them there or not.

If I reflect upon my experience negatively, I conclude that Western civilization is dying. Things are not the way they once were. Contemporary life is decadent. The Christian values that I once acknowledged publicly are challenged within society and often appear to be only conflicting opinions. The media headlines suggest to me that, given the perpetual state of war and conflict in which the world is engaged, world destruction is possible. The moral principles that formerly held my life together seem to be disintegrating as the traditional supports of my life–world and the given world are undermined.

However, if I reflect on my experience positively, the universe goes on because I am a cheerful and optimistic person. I believe that life is good and I sense that I am a part of a larger rhythm of creation. In fact, I am more than a part of that creation. I am a co–creator of that creation, both in the present and in the future. In my personal and public life I have expressed this optimistic attitude through my religious conviction and ordained ministry.

Individuals often accept religion as but one cultural and sociological component among others. These include the philosophical, political and economic movements which are social constructions and which have characterized human development throughout the ages. Each of these social constructions has come about through human activity. It must be remembered that no human activity, whether religious, philosophical, political or economic requires any necessary system of interpretation. There are interpretive options. Further, no philosophical activity produces permanent facts but only provides temporary understanding that is contingent upon the cultural facts in which the thinking takes place.

As soon as I give any meaning to my experience I enter the realm of philosophy, either formally in a tutored sense or informally through common sense. Philosophy is a contemplative activity reserved to humans living in society. To the best of my current philosophical awareness, there is at least agreement that brute animals cannot attribute meaning to their experiences. Humans, however, can do that. Members of human societies and institutions intentionally relate themselves to each other within the environment that is common to them.

As a human, then, my theological insights are the fruit of my philosophical contemplation of the revelation of God within the church community. The church, which is constituted of individuals who are "called out" of the general human population, exists in response to a divine summons regardless of any particular cultural milieu. Thus, the church as a "called out" community provides the unique *locus* for the interpretation of God's revelation.

Yet, it must be remembered that the church does not exhaust the total People of God. The church as a social institution is the means whereby individuals are able to relate themselves religiously to each other. Further, it must be remembered that the decay or the growth of any social institution, the church included, will have a corresponding effect on those individuals constituting that institution. My experience has been that the church cannot constitute itself in the defensive and self–isolating context of decay. Rather, the opposite is required. The church must constitute itself as a self–constituting community open to future growth as the People of God.

So, it is that my phenomenological philosophy, which supports my theology, has taken on the unique characteristic of personal self–discovery. Phenomenological philosophy satisfies my personal needs when: 1) its purpose arises from within my actual experience, 2) its purpose is to serve a definite function of spiritual growth, and 3) its purpose is supported by my community.

POSTSCRIPT

Only after this book was completed and shortly before it was published, I obtained a copy of *Leaves from the Note Book of an Unashamed Heretic* by Paul Trudinger. Paul had taught me at the University of Winnipeg in a postgraduate programme in theology which I never completed. I recall how "unorthodox" his approach to theological issues seemed to be to us students. In hindsight, I believe he was undertaking his own version of the dehellenization process based on experience rather than philosophical critique. As the reader will no doubt have recognized, the dehellenization notion I presented in this book is understood within the Catholic Christian point of view. This is the tradition in which I was educated and taught to practice my faith. However, Christians of other traditions, like Paul Trudinger, may undertake a process of dehellenization in their religious lives without labeling it as such. Where I have focused on philosophy, Trudinger, a Quaker, has focused on personal experience. He writes:

> If I were pressed to say in one short statement how I would describe the shift in my thinking and convictions, I would say it was a movement away from a strong 'Christocentric' focus to the conviction that 'God' must always be at the center.... In former days I would have hotly denied that having 'God' at the center required any weakening of my Christology. As I now understand things, my former Christocentric perspective carried with it particular constructions, interpretations, and understandings of 'God' – constructions which I now think, feel and believe to be unhelpful, and in many cases downright damaging, to our understanding of the relationship of God to humankind. I would not even call the shift one from a 'Christocentric' to a 'Theocentic' position, because God as *Theos,* that is, the classical *theistic* position carries with it a model of God which, I believe, fosters the

ideas of domination, of triumphalism, of hierarchy, and of authoritarian attitudes. These I believe to be unhelpful in our present situation in history; in our current sensitivity to religious pluralism and multi-culturalism. I do not find such a view of God to be operative in my own spiritual experience of God personally speaking, nor in the context of the communities of faith when they are being faithful to Love's presence and to the spirit of Jesus' life and teaching. [4]

---

[4] Trudinger, Paul (1988). *Leaves from the Notebook of an Unashamed Heretic.* Kingston, ON: Frye & Company.

REFERENCE LIST

Anthony, Louise (2007). *Philosophers Without Gods: Meditations on Atheism and the Secular Life.* New York: Oxford University Press.

Brandt, Richard (1941). *The Philosophy of Schleiermacher. The Development of His Theory of Scientific and Religious Knowledge.* New York: Harper & Brothers, (p. 55).

Davis, Charles (1967). *A Question of Conscience.* London: Hodder & Stoughton.

Fabel, Arthur, "Teilhard de Chardin and the New Scientific Synthesis," in *The Desire to be Human: A Global Reconnaissance of Human Perspectives in an Age of Transformation Written in Honour of Pierre Teilhard de Chardin,* eds. Leo Zonneveld and Robert Muller. The Netherlands: Mirananda, 1983, (p. 87).

Flannery, Austin (1996). *The Basic Sixteen Documents of Vatican Council II: Constitutions and Decrees.* New York: Costello.

Giorgi, Amedeo (2008). "Difficulties Encountered in the Application of the Phenomenological Method in the Social Sciences," in *The Indo–Pacific Journal of Phenomenology,* Vol. 8, Edition 1 (May).

Guerrière, Daniel (1990). *Phenomenology of the Truth Proper to Religion.* New York: State University of New York Press.

Henderson–Davis, Claire (2007). *After the Church: Divine Encounter in a Sexual Age.* Norwich: Canterbury Press.

Kobler, John, "Vatican II Theology Needs Discussion," *The Modern Schoolman* 78, no. 1 (2000).

Laycock, Stephen William (1986). "Introduction Toward an Overview of Phenomenological Theology," in *Essays in Phenomenological Theology,* eds. Laycock & Hart, (New York: State University Press of New York).

Macann, Christopher, "Being and Becoming" in *Philosophy Now* (Dec. 2016/Jan. 2017) https://philosophynow.org (accessed 16 Dec. 2016).

Murry, J. Middleton (1927). *The Evolution of the Intellectual.* London: Jonathan Cape.

O'Murchu, Diramuid (2000). *Religion in Exile. A Spiritual Homecoming.* New York: Crossroad.

Sabatier, Auguste (2003) [1904?]. *Religions of Authority and the Religion of the Spirit.* Whitefish, MT: Kessinger Publishing Reprint.

Sagovsky, Nicholas (1990). *On God's Side. A Life of George Tyrrell.* Oxford. Clarendon Press.

Schillebeeckx, Edward (1967). *Revelation and Theology.* London: Sheed and Ward (Stagbooks).

—, Edward (1984). *The Schillebeeckx Reader,* ed. Robert Schreiter, (New York: Crossroad).

Schlick, Moritz (1938). "Form and Content, an Introduction to Philosophical Thinking," in *Gesammelte Aufsatze, 1926-1936.* Vienna: Gerold, pp 117–34. First published in *College of the Pacific Publications in Philosophy I,* 1932, (pp. 45-62).

Schultenover, David (1981). *George Tyrrell: In Search of Catholicism.* Shepherdstown, New York: Patmos.

Segesvary, Victor (2003). *World State, Nation States, or Non-Centralized Institutions? A Vision of the Future in Politics.* Lanham, MD: University Press of America.

Smuts, J. C. (1926). *Holism and Evolution.* New York: Macmillan.

Stöckl, K (2007). "Community after Totalitarianism: The Eastern Orthodox Intellectual Tradition and the Philosophical Discourse of Political Modernity." Doctor of Political Science Dissertation, European University Institute.

Strasser, Stephan (1963). *Phenomenology and the Human Sciences: A Contribution to a New Scientific Ideal.* Editions E. Nauwelaerts, Louvain. (Duquesne University Psychological Studies 1).

Thomas, E. E. (1938). *The Political Aspect of Religious Development.* London: Heritage and Unicorn Press (pp. 183–90).

Tyrrell, George (1906). *Lex Credendi: A Sequel to Lex Orandi.* London: Longmans.

—, George (1910). *The Church and the Future.* London: Priory Press.

—, George (1912). *Autobiography and Life of George Tyrrell in Two Volumes.* London: Edward Arnold.

Weaver, Mary Jo (1981). *Letters from A Modernist: The Letters of George Tyrrell to Wilfrid Ward 1893-1908.* London: Sheed & Ward.

Wells, David (1981). *The Prophetic Theology of George Tyrrell.* Chico, CA: Scholars Press.

ABOUT THE AUTHOR

ALLAN SAVAGE, ordained Catholic priest in 1978, is now retired from active ministry. Having co–authored books with various others, George Drazenovich, Erik Mansager, Sheldon Nicholl, and Peter Stuart, he continues with his writing career in philosophy and theology. A life-long learner he has obtained doctoral degrees from the University of South Africa, the St. Elias School of Orthodox Theology and the European–American University, now The Western Orthodox University. His ministry has included pastoral work in parishes, hospitals and diocesan offices, as well as teaching as sessional lecturer in the former Faculty of Theology at the University of Winnipeg, which in 2013, became The United Centre for Theological Studies.

www.allansavage.org

ENDNOTES

[1] Edward Schillebeeckx (1967:284) makes a similar comment with respect to theologians. "It is always instructive to find out how great theologians went to work in their own time, not in order to imitate them, but so that we may also do, independently, in our own time what they did in theirs."

[2] Tyrrell, George (1912: Vol.1: 119).

[3] Edward Schillebeeckx (1967: 99) writes: "A theological study was therefore, for Aquinas, a study concerned with the 'first cause' of things, whereas a philosophical study was concerned with things in their own value."

[4] Alfred Firmin Loisy (1857–1940) was a French Roman Catholic priest, professor and theologian who became the intellectual standard bearer for Biblical Modernism in the Roman Catholic Church. He was a critic of traditional views of the biblical accounts of creation, and argued that biblical criticism could be applied to interpreting scripture. His theological positions brought him into conflict with the Church's conservatives, including Pope Leo XIII and Pope Pius X. In 1893, he was dismissed as a professor from the Catholic Institute of Paris. His books were condemned by the Vatican and in 1908 he was excommunicated.

[5] Daniel Guerrière (1990:13) is of the same view and writes that progress in philosophy is better understood through *ressourcement* rather than an advancement in thought.

[6] In her book, *After the Church: Divine Encounter in a Sexual Age,* Claire Henderson–Davis provides a perspective on theological thinking that is not ecclesiastical, but ecclesial. In my review of her book I wrote: "In 'grappling with the meaning of life in a Western post–Christian world' (Rosemary Ruether), Claire's short work is not to be mistaken for an average self–help book. It is an example of contemporary practice of theologizing "outside the church," as she admits. Though short, the book contains pithy, insightful comments arising out of personal experience. The book gives the impression that almost every word is weighed. The enduring value of this work,

to my mind, is that Claire invites us to follow her parents' decision in our respective lives. "They stopped reading the story and stepped into the book" to find a new imaging of God. My initial reading was completed in one afternoon. However, the more enriching reading followed over the period of a few days. I had purchased the book on speculation that I might gain some insight into her father's theological understanding since I am doing research for a book on the theological similarities and differences among Charles Davis, Leslie Dewart and Gregory Baum. I read this book as a philosopher, but not presupposing any particular school, i.e., Thomist, Cartesian, Hegelian, etc. so as not to prejudice my appreciation of her perspective. Were I to discern a philosophy underpinning her thinking, I would identify it as holistic phenomenology. Whether one's point of departure in reading the book is as a philosopher, a theologian, a social critic, or a wounded soul, there are brief personal statements throughout the book that reveal a great deal about her fidelity to revelation in relating her growth through a variety of human personal experiences. If I have understood her correctly, I draw the conclusion that for some of us we may have to "leave the church" in order to "enter the Church" and leave the guilt behind. [The proposed book on Davis, Dewart and Baum was never written.]

[7] Charles Davis was ordained Catholic priest in the year I was born — 1946. He was a product of his intellectual and religious times, like all of us are. I became aware of the similarity of our intentions only after he had died and recall contacting his daughter, Claire Henderson–Davis, living in England, about memories of her father. Sadly, any and all correspondence I had with her has been lost. The following is abstracted from Davis's Epilogue to his *A Question of Conscience* (1967:240).

"Throughout the book my aim has been to give as honest an explanation as I could of the reasons, both negative and positive, which led me to leave the Roman Catholic Church. I have hidden nothing of which I have been conscious.

Nor have I tried to work up my case *post factum*. I am writing these last lines in the middle of June 1967, not yet six months since I publicly announced my decision. I have done practically no reading directly for this book. I wanted to record for myself and for others the state of mind in which I made my break with the Roman Church.

I have not attempted to be other than my usual self as a theologian. I can see well enough that the fundamental intellectual problems for Christians today are the problem of our knowledge of God in relation to modern theology and the question of the uniqueness of Christ in the confrontation with the other world religions. But for reasons I have explained I regard *the immediate problem* as that of the Church, the solution of which will place Christians in a situation where they can tackle *the other problems* on the basis of a freely developing Christian tradition [italics Savage]. The Church was in any case the problem that faced me, and personal thought must arise from one's own personal situation.

So now I leave my book. I want to learn from others. I have no wish to forestall criticism, but there is a danger when much is at stake of imitating Bossuet, who, according to Friedrich Heer, 'was a perfect man of the baroque, preserving what he knew was false because he was afraid of what might replace it.'"

Davis died in 1999.